Made 4 More

Leading a Life Well Lived

- Family
- Personal
- Spiritual
- Financial
- Community

STEVE CHADER

For permission requests, write to the publisher, addressed "Attention: Permissions Coordinator," reception@markvictorhansenlibrary.com

Quantity sales special discounts are available on quantity purchases by corporations, associations, and others. For details, contact the publisher at reception@markvictorhansenlibrary.com

Orders by U.S. trade bookstores and wholesalers. Email: reception@markvictorhansenlibrary.com

Creative Contributors - Mike Valentino and Carol McManus
Book Layout and Cover Design - DBree

Manufactured and printed in the United States of America distributed globally by markvictorhansenlibrary.com

MVHL

New York | Los Angeles | London | Sydney

ISBN: 979-8-88581-214-6 Hardback
ISBN: 979-8-88581-215-3 Paperback
ISBN: 979-8-88581-216-0 eBook
Library of Congress Control Number: 2025919144

Dedication

This book is dedicated to two people without whose support this book would not have been possible.

Jill Chader
My wife, you provided a stable foundation for our family and kept the home fires burning while I was out learning and serving others.

Jennice Doty
My business partner and friend for more than thirty years. You encouraged me to start, and to continue this journey of growth.

Testimonials

"Made 4 More is a powerful reminder that we are meant to live with purpose, passion, and intentional growth in every area of life. Through engaging storytelling and timeless wisdom, Steve Chader shows how abundance is built through relationships, resilience, and values. Inspiring, practical, and deeply life-affirming."

— Brandon Barnum
CEO, HOA.com

$\infty\infty$

"For more than 25 years, I've known Steve as a leader who not only teaches principles of success but lives them every day. We've served together on the KW Cares Board of Directors, and I've repeatedly entrusted him to lead our annual leadership clinics as a faculty member of Keller Williams University. At Keller Williams, our mission is "to build a life worth living." The timeless lessons and powerful story Steve shares in this book will not just inspire you — they'll equip you to create that life for yourself."

— Mo Anderson
Former CEO of Keller Williams Realty International

$\infty\infty$

"In this book Steve teaches a way of thinking about life that results in taking the right actions to achieve our ideal life of abundance. Through its story, Steve shows just how easy it is to get distracted and mistakenly miss the bigger picture and he reminds us that in the end, an abundant life simply requires intentional growth."

— Gary Keller
Founder, Keller Williams Realty
Bestselling Author, *The One Thing*

⦿⦿⦿⦿

"As a reader of Made 4 More: Leading a Life Well-Lived, I was deeply moved by its message and reminded of the value of relationships. This isn't just a book you read; it's a book you live. Through the relatable struggles and triumphs of its characters, it beautifully illustrates how to navigate the complexities of life— from career setbacks and health scares to finding purpose and community.

The concept of the 5 interconnected circles is a powerful framework for self-reflection, abundance, growth and relationships. It's a gentle yet profound reminder that a truly abundant life isn't about having everything, but about how we think, the environment we allow and the people we prioritize. I walked away from this book not only with a renewed sense of hope but with practical ideas for living with more intention and authenticity. This is a must-read for anyone who feels stuck and is ready to start building a life of true purpose and connection."

— Bruce Hardie

⦿⦿⦿⦿

"In Made 4 More, Steve Chader masterfully distills the essence of what it means to live a fulfilling life. His powerful leadership principles resonate deeply, guiding readers to focus on what truly matters. This book is not just a collection of insights; it's a transformative journey that encourages us to redefine success beyond mere achievement. Through relatable stories and actionable wisdom, Steve invites us to cultivate abundance in our relationships and lives. If you're seeking a compass to navigate your unique path to fulfillment, this book shows the way."

— J'aime Nowak

"This book is an invitation to look at your mindset and realize that the way you think shapes the way you live. Steve reminds us that we aren't stuck. Our context — the filter through which we see the world — can be changed, stretched, and expanded. And when it does, so does everything else in our lives.

I've seen it in my own journey. Early in my real estate career, I had to learn that success wasn't just about working harder, true success required thinking differently. Changing my environment, having higher level conversations, and learning from those who had gone before me (Steve in many cases) completely transformed how I showed up as a Realtor, a business owner, a leader, a wife, a mom and just as a person in general. What Steve gives you here is that same gift: the tools, stories, and faith-filled truths that shift your mindset toward abundance.

I love that through the story this book points back to what really matters: faith over fear, growth over scarcity, gratitude that overflows and blesses others. That's what an abundant life is made of. Made 4 More doesn't just give you ideas, it equips you with simple steps to put them into action so you can start living that way now.

If you're ready to think bigger, grow into the best version of yourself and step into the life God designed for you, then this is your book. Because the truth is — you were Made 4 More."

— Christin Kingsbury

"Steve Chader's wisdom reminds us that a life well lived is built in the 5 circles: family, personal, financial, spiritual, and community. This book is a timeless guide for anyone seeking balance, purpose, and impact."

— Linda McKissack
Bestselling Author and Entrepreneur

"*Steve Chader has been one of the most influential leaders in my life. He helped reframe my thinking in ways I could not have reached on my own, giving language and clarity to principles I was already striving to live by but could never quite articulate. The idea of abundance in every area of life has been so compelling that it became foundational for me, woven into our family, our family banking business, and the way we run our company Factum Financial.*

What Steve writes about in Made 4 More is not theory, he lives this out personally, and it is exactly what so many people in this world are searching for. Of all the areas, the spiritual circle is the most important, and Steve's work has helped me anchor everything else to it. Steve has been like a father figure to me, and I believe with all my heart that our connection was no coincidence, but one of God's instances. This book is a gift, and I cannot recommend it enough."

— Kyle Fuller

"*Finally! Steve has put into one book what it's taken me 50 years of reading self-help, inspirational, and business-building books to piece together. He's been teaching these ideas for years, and I've always wished he'd share them with the world—and now he has. As you read, you'll find defining moments that feel so familiar to your own life, along with action steps that make the path to happiness and success really clear.*

Well done, Partner—this is exactly the message people need."

— Jennice Doty
Owner/Broker TCT Property Management Services

"My dear friend Steve Chader gives us this beautiful reminder that, this is our life. We can breath into it, in new ways that allows us the full experience, if we choose. This book is a spark. It lights the way, lays out the inspiration, and then give us the tools. So many are searching right now. This could not be written at a better time."

— Bev Steiner

"This book offers a powerful reminder that a life well-lived is intentionally designed through becoming the person you were meant to be, finding growth and balance in all 5 areas of your life: Family, Personal, Community, Financial, Spiritual. The roadmap to a growth mindset for an abundant life."

— Larry Lloyd

Preface

Welcome!! My name is Steve Chader, and I want to thank you for reading this book. Why should you? Because I believe that once you start thinking about the ideas presented here, your life will change in good ways you may not have yet imagined.

This is a story about people who could be just like you and me. It's about life, leadership and lessons learned. Our lives are comprised of 5 separate and interconnected areas. Spiritual, Personal, Family, Financial and Community. If that's true, and I believe it is, then what?

I like to think about each area as a circle. A circle is continuous. It doesn't have a beginning or an end, and it can grow or shrink. The direction or size it takes depends on how you lead. Some people lead their life intentionally, while others live a life of default. In other words, some only react to what happens while others have a vision for more. Vision for what they want life to look like and then they intentionally move in that direction. That's called leadership.

I believe we are created for abundance in each of the 5 areas. My definition of abundance is "I have what I need, and there is more". You and I were created for more. While grateful for what we have, knowing there's more, we choose to intentionally grow in that direction. Each of us has certain passions in various areas. That's why we go to school to learn to think, take lessons in things we love like music or golf, develop more skills, serve others, spend time with loved ones. This list is endless.

Each person on this earth has a purpose. There is an old saying, "The best day of your life is when you were born. The next best day is when you find out why."

Eleanor Roosevelt is quoted as saying, "Great minds talk about ideas. Average minds talk about events. Small minds talk about people." I choose to talk about the following ideas.

1. Leading a Life Well Lived.

2. Life includes 5 separate and interconnected circles

3. The ideal life is abundance in each circle.

4. The most important thing in each circle is relationships

5. Abundance requires intentional growth.

I pray this book will be a steppingstone for you to enhance your leadership and build your ability to create a life of abundance. More cherished relationships, more peace and joy, more gratitude, more generosity, more fabulous experiences, and more happiness. There is More. You were created to enjoy it.

Contents

Chapter One

Kristin Marchan never imagined that moving into a luxurious new home in New Canaan would leave her feeling more restless than fulfilled. On the surface, everything was perfect: a beautiful house, two well-behaved German Shepherds, and a devoted husband with a thriving career in Manhattan. But as the days passed in quiet solitude, she found herself wandering from room to room, her thoughts louder than the surrounding silence.

On a bright Tuesday morning, she jogged alongside her friend, Amy, through a winding two-mile hiking trail. Both women were in great shape, easily outpacing the rising heat. As they emerged onto the main road, Amy challenged, "Race you to the gazebo."

Without a word, Kristin put her head down and

broke into a sprint. Amy did the same and caught up with her friend in an instant. As they raced ahead, a flock of Canada geese scattered to get out of their way. Amy's long legs gave her a clear advantage, but Kristin offset the disparity with sheer energy. She bolted past Amy just as they reached the freshly painted gazebo, leaping up the steps and across the "finish line."

Leaning over to catch her breath, Amy panted, "Are you on some kind of super vitamin?"

Kristin grinned but didn't answer. They sat down on a nearby bench overlooking a pond where a family of geese floated lazily. "It's not vitamins," Kristin said. "It's boredom."

"Boredom? How does that make you run faster?"

"It doesn't," Kristin replied. "But spending so much time jogging around my neighborhood and getting on the Stairmaster every day because I have nothing else to do gives my legs a great workout."

Kristin went on to share about her posh but isolating lifestyle since her husband Justin began commuting daily into Manhattan for his high-powered job. Though she was grateful for their new home and the wealth that came with an inheritance from Justin's late grandfather, she felt increasingly unfulfilled. "I know it sounds ungrateful," she said, "but I just want to be more than the wife of a rich guy."

Amy, her childhood friend from their modest

neighborhood in South Windsor, nodded. "So do something about it. You've got the time and resources. There's nothing stopping you."

Kristin hesitated. "Actually, I've had an idea for a while. I just haven't said it out loud before."

Amy encouraged her, and Kristin shared her dream of opening a dog daycare and training center—right in her backyard. "I've always loved animals. It's the one thing that really excites me."

"Then go for it, Kris. What have you got to lose?"

Kristin burst out laughing. "I don't think Justin will like the idea. It's not that he doesn't support me. He's just proud that I don't have to work because he's so successful."

"Do you know what that sounds like?" Amy challenged. "This is not 1950, and you are not June Cleaver wearing pearls around your neck while you vacuum the living room."

"I know. I'm a modern woman living in a gorgeous home in one of the wealthiest communities in America. I have a terrific husband who loves me. And yet, it just feels like everything in my life is out of whack. Is that crazy or what?"

"You know I'm always here for you, but I have a better idea. Do you know who Benjamin Pike is?"

Kristin shook her head as she swiped the sweat from her water bottle across her forehead.

"He's this really cool guy, a longtime local figure who speaks locally at Chamber of Commerce events and even informal coffee meetups. Ben says the ideal life is built around having abundance in 5 areas of your life—spiritual, personal, family, financial and community."

Kristin sniffed, "Yeah, okay. So, what does that have to do with me?"

"Everything, Kris. Don't you see? The reason you're feeling out of whack is because those things aren't in balance."

"I agree. That makes sense. Does he have a book, or do you know when he's speaking again? I'll try anything."

"Don't know about a book, but I do know he loves to sit and chat with people. I've met with him myself." Amy dug out her phone and typed. "I just sent you his contact information. Reach out and tell him I said to call."

"You really think I should talk with him?"

Amy nodded, "Every time I speak with him, I walk away thinking clearer than when I got there. He listens like he's known you forever."

"Okay. What have I got to lose?" Kristin stood and signaled for Amy to follow. They enjoyed a comfortable jog in silence as they headed back to their cars.

Before driving away, Amy called out. "Make sure you call Ben today."

"I will. I promise."

Kristin didn't waste any time. Right after her shower, still feeling the energy from her conversation with Amy, she sent a quick text message to Benjamin Pike. It was informal, just a request to meet up and "pick his brain," as she put it. To her surprise, he responded within the hour, suggesting they meet for coffee that afternoon at his favorite café in downtown New Canaan.

The place was charming and quiet, filled with the aroma of roasted beans and fresh pastries. When Kristin walked in, she spotted a man in the back sitting by himself at the corner table. His tousled salt and pepper hair gave him the image of a kindly professor. He was wearing a light blue sweater over a collared shirt. He waved, and the warm twinkle in his eyes somehow put her at ease.

Ben stood and they shook hands. "I'm Benjamin Pike, but please call me Ben." He pulled out the chair for her and then returned to his seat.

"I appreciate you making the time for me. I'm Kristin Marchan. Amy Newhouse told me about you and said we should meet."

"Of course," Ben said. "Any friend of Amy is a friend of mine."

The waitress came and took their orders. While they waited for her to bring their lattes, Ben asked Kristin to tell him about herself. She was surprised as the words tumbled out like coins dropping from a slot machine. In a matter of minutes, she had shared details about where she grew up, how she met Justin, what he did for a living, and why they chose to live in New Canaan.

The waitress placed the mugs on the table. "Anything else?"

Ben replied. "No, we're in good shape. Thanks Steph."

Kristin lifted the steaming, foam-filled mug to her lips. "I can't believe I just shared all that. I hope I didn't bore you."

Ben laughed. "Not at all. I love getting to know people."

"So, I don't want to do all the talking. Tell me about yourself," Kristin said.

Ben proceeded to tell her he was a retired schoolteacher and lived on a small farm just north of New Canaan in Pound Ridge, NY. "I have a pretty good-sized apple orchard and a few peach trees. My wife passed about six years ago, and now it's just me and Jake and Molly, my faithful Irish Setters."

Kristin laughed, "I'm a dog person too. Mine are German Shepherds, Zeus and Thor. Their names sound ferocious, but they're big old love bugs."

Ben continued to tease out Kristin's story and over the next hour learned of her boredom and dreams about opening a dog daycare and training center. She intimated her sense of feeling aimless and desire to do something more meaningful than being a Wall Street wife.

"I want my life to matter."

Ben listened closely. He didn't interrupt, didn't judge. He simply nodded, offering the occasional "mmhmm" or "go on."

"We have almost 5 acres, and I don't think it will violate any zoning." She paused, "Do you think I'm crazy?"

He stroked his chin and spoke, his voice a deep, rich baritone. "Dreams are never crazy. The more vivid they are, the more likely they are to come true. What's holding you back?"

Kristin shrugged. "I don't know. I've never done anything like this before, but I feel like I have to try . . . for me. Do you know what I mean?"

"I think your instincts are pointing you in the right direction," he said. "The key to a well-lived life is abundance—but it's not just about money. It's about fulfillment across all 5 areas that affect our lives."

"Amy told me a little about that. Can you explain it to me?"

"I'll give you the quick overview. We are all created for a purpose. The journey in life is to discover what your purpose is. And fulfillment in life is when your activities align with who you were created to be. Abundance in life requires intentional growth in these 5 critical areas. They are spiritual, personal, family, financial, and community. From what you've told me, you've already got a handle on some of them. You just need to connect them all."

Kristin's eyes lit up. "That's a lot to digest, but it's exactly what I needed to hear." She drew her finger across the rim of the coffee mug. "I was worried I would sound silly to someone like you."

Ben chuckled. "There's nothing silly about wanting your life to matter. I'm sure your husband would agree. What does he think about your idea?"

"Justin? I haven't told him yet. I know he wants me to be happy, but he thinks it's his job to make me happy."

"I suspect you already know that happiness comes from within. I'm sure Justin knows that too."

"I guess so. I'm pretty sure he'll support whatever I decide to do."

By the time they finished their second round of coffee, Kristin felt like something inside her was beginning to emerge. It wasn't just about starting a business anymore—it was about shaping a life she could be proud of. She thanked Ben and promised to keep him updated.

"I'll be cheering you on," he said. "And if you ever need another sounding board, you know where to find me."

Later that week, Kristin texted Ben and asked if she could pay him a visit . I'd love to see your apple orchard. Do you have time today?

He texted back. Come by anytime. I'm home all day.

When she arrived, she found him tending to his apple trees just behind the house. He stepped off the ladder and greeted her with a fatherly bear hug. Molly and Jake came bounding from the porch to greet the new visitor. Ben laughed, "I'm so glad you came and obviously, so are my housemates."

Kristin leaned down and gave each dog a scratch behind the ear and asked Ben if she could give them a treat.

"I think they'd be very disappointed if you didn't. You three settle on the porch and I'll bring us some iced tea." He disappeared before she could respond.

Once settled into the matching wicker rockers, Ben and Kristin lapsed into another long conversation about living an abundant life and how to achieve it. She was a bit surprised by how eager he was to sit and talk again, but grateful for his willingness to share his wisdom.

"When we met the other day, you talked about the 5 circles," she began. "I can't stop thinking about it."

Ben smiled warmly. "That's usually a good sign."

"I know I want to start something new," Kristin said,

explaining more details about her dog care idea. "But I don't want it to be just a business. I want it to mean something."

Ben offered a simple but powerful response: "Purpose leads. The rest follows. If this brings meaning to your life—and serves others—that's worth building."

He shared stories from his own life. How loss had shaped him. How his orchard wasn't just about apples but about creating something sustainable for future generations. "The abundant life doesn't mean having everything. It means building something that matters in every part of your life."

"I'm beginning to understand that. I talked to Justin about my ideas, and I shared what you told me about living an abundant life."

"I can tell by the pinched look on your face that maybe he's not on board yet."

"Yes and no. He says I should do what makes me happy. But I'm not sure he grasped the idea. He needs to live a life of abundance, too, right?"

"That is my fervent hope for everyone. Would it be helpful if I met with you and Justin together?"

"I'd love that, but I don't think he'd agree . . . at least not yet. But thanks for offering."

Kristin left their meeting energized. She wasn't just starting a business. She was stepping into a calling. All she had to do was figure out how to do it and how to get Justin to go along.

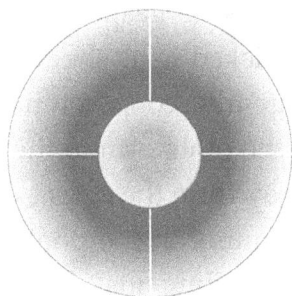

Chapter Two

Pamela Stephens headed inside the house, the coolness of the central air conditioning a sharp contrast to the blazing heat outside. As she made her way through the living room and into her large kitchen, she heard a shrill scream from out back. Her heart skipped a beat. "Suzy!" she exclaimed.

Spinning around and racing back through the sliding glass door, the panicked woman heard the ruckus. She stopped short, taking in the scene; two enormous German Shepherds were ten feet from her grandchildren, barking at full volume. Her granddaughter, Suzy cowered underneath one of the lounge chairs while her grandson, Sammy stood tall, trying to act brave, but all the color had drained from his face. Pamela watched with wide eyes as one of the dogs started forward, and Sammy took a few steps backwards, falling into the deep end of the pool.

The boy flailed as he gasped for breath. Pamela's lifeguard instincts kicked in as she made a mad dash to the pool, leapt in, gently scooped him up with one arm as she swam with the other arm to the ladder on the far side of the pool away from the dogs.

As she lifted Sammy to the pool deck, she spotted a young woman standing just inside the fence. She looked to be in her late twenties, with medium-length dirty blonde hair tied up in a bun and wearing stylish-looking cut-offs and a tank top. "Zeus. Thor," the woman commanded. "Come!"

Instantly, the dogs stopped barking and ran, dropping to the ground at her feet. The woman spoke to the young girl trembling underneath the lounge chair. "It's OK, sweetie, they're very friendly. They won't hurt you."

Suzy remained right where she was until Pamela reached the chair and coaxed her out. Sammy was one step behind his grandmother. She put an arm around his shoulder and pulled Suzy into a hug. "You kids go inside."

"But Grammy . . ." Sammy started.

"Please, Sammy, do as I say." Her voice gave no room for argument. "You too, Suzy. And close the door. Everything will be fine."

The kids scurried for the door; their eyes never leaving the dogs.

Pamela turned her attention toward the stranger; the

two dogs still in a prone position. "I just need to speak with this nice lady for a moment," her tone not half as pleasant as her words.

Once the kids were safely inside, Pamela walked over to her unexpected visitor, looking her right in the eye. She ignored the pair of now docile dogs.

"I am so sorry," the contrite woman said. "I know the dogs can look intimidating, but I assure you, the kids were never in any danger."

Pamela retorted, "I beg to differ. My grandson fell into the pool; if I hadn't jumped in, he could have drowned."

The young woman looked embarrassed. "You're right. You're absolutely right," she conceded. "I promise it will never happen again."

The pair of canines looked up at Pamela, their eyes bright and their demeanor calm. "May I pet them?"

"Of course. Zeus, Thor, say hello to our neighbor."

Pamela leaned down and held out the back of her hand for them to sniff. They responded with an amicable lick to her wrist. "I actually love dogs," Pamela said in a more conciliatory voice. "And these are beautiful animals. What are their names again?"

With a smile, the newcomer said, "They are Zeus and Thor." She offered her slender hand and added, "And I'm Kristin Marchan. My husband, Justin, and I moved into the neighborhood recently."

They shook hands. "I'm Pamela Stephens. That's right; we saw the moving van. I was planning to come over and welcome you to the neighborhood, but . . . well . . . I guess I should have done that sooner."

With a pleasant laugh, Kristin said, "I guess the boys here beat you to it," gesturing to the two dogs. "Again, I'm so sorry they came running over here like that and scared your kids. They haven't learned the boundaries of our property yet."

"Grandkids," Pamela corrected.

"Really? You don't look old enough to be a grandmother."

"Keep complimenting me like that and we're going to be best friends," Pamela chuckled. "I'd ask you to stay for tea, but I think I better get inside and check on the kids."

"I understand. Maybe we can do a rain check." Kristin snapped her fingers and pointed to the fence. The dogs stood and ran ahead, waiting until she unlatched the gate. The trio disappeared, and Pamela went back to the house where Sammy and Suzy were waiting, their noses pressed against the glass.

"Are they gone?" Suzy asked.

"Yes, and just so you know, they are friendly dogs, and Mrs. Marchan is our new neighbor. We'll find another time to reintroduce you to them, and I'll bet Zeus and Thor will be your best friends."

Sammy looked skeptical. "But they're so big, and they bark a lot." Suzy nodded in agreement.

"I guarantee the next time they visit it will be different. But that's not today. What do you say we go take a dip in the pool?" Pamela urged.

They spent the next hour in the water with their grandmother close by.

(((())))

Marcus arrived home at 5:30. The house was quiet now. Sammy and Suzy's mom picked them up at four, giving Pamela just enough time to take a shower and change before starting dinner.

Marcus loosened his tie as soon as he came into the kitchen from the garage. He kissed his wife on the cheek and headed for the living room, where he plunked down in his favorite recliner. Pamela followed. "Have a tough day, dear?

"No worse than usual," he replied. "It's just that I've been working a lot lately, and I'm not as young as I used to be. How about you?" he asked. "Did you have fun with the kids today?"

Pamela sat down on the sofa next to his chair. "Funny you should ask."

"Was there a problem?" he frowned.

Pamela shook her head. "No, they're fine," she said,

"but we did have an interesting visit from our new neighbor."

"Oh, the people that bought the Milroy's house?"

"Yes," she replied. "But what happened was kind of disturbing. I went into the house to get lunch, and when I came out, there were these two huge dogs barking at the kids, and . . ."

"Oh my God! Were they hurt?" His eyes blazed with alarm.

She leaned forward and patted his knee. "No, nothing like that. They're fine. They were just scared." Pamela went on to tell him about the two German Shepherds and how she jumped in the pool to save Sammy.

Marcus stood, his face beet red. "He could have drowned! What is wrong with those people?"

"To be honest, honey, the young woman . . . her name is Kristin, I think . . . was very apologetic. It was just an accident. She promised it will never happen again."

"Well, it better not. And I'm going to see that it doesn't." He started for the door.

"Where are you going?" she called after him.

"I'm going to give these people a piece of my mind," he snarled, slamming the door behind him. She raced to stop him, but by the time she got to the porch, he was already past the end of the drive.

Marcus marched up the long driveway that led to the ornate front door of the palatial colonial home. It was impressive even by the standards of their affluent neighborhood. He pressed the doorbell. The ringing tone was accompanied by the barking of dogs on high alert.

Kristin Marchan opened the heavy door. "May I help you?" she asked. The dogs raced forward, and Marcus took a step back. She snapped her fingers, and the dogs immediately sat at attention, flanking her sides.

"My name is Marcus Stephens. My wife, Pamela, said there was some sort of incident at my home today involving your dogs."

"Yes, there was Mr. Stephens, and as I told your wife, I am so sorry. It won't happen again."

"So, it was your dogs that nearly mauled my grandchildren!"

"No. They never got that close to the kids. They only barked and scared them."

Just then, a young man with a stubble beard emerged from down a hallway. The sleeves on his expensive-looking white dress shirt were rolled up just above his thick forearms. He stepped in front of his wife. "I'll handle this, Kris." He turned his attention to the man standing on the porch. "Who are you and why are you harassing my wife?"

Kristin said, "Honey, he wasn't . . ."

The man put up his hand. "Please, Kris. I'll handle this. Now, did I hear this has something to do with our dogs?"

Marcus did not flinch at the man's aggressive tone.

"It certainly does. They came into my yard and scared the heck out of my grandchildren. My young grandson fell into the pool." He made firm eye contact, and the two seemed to be daring each other to blink. Marcus continued, "If your dogs come onto my property again, I'm going to contact the town's animal control officer and file a formal complaint."

Justin Marchan shot back through gritted teeth. "I don't appreciate being threatened."

Marcus let out a deep breath. "Look, it's my turn to apologize. Maybe I overreacted. There's no need for this situation to get out of control," he said, trying to cool down the temperature of the conversation. "I'm sure you can appreciate how protective a grandfather can be."

Justin did not respond, so he continued. "We didn't get off to a good start as neighbors, but it shouldn't stay that way." Marcus extended his hand. "I'm Marcus Stephens. I hope we all agree it was an unfortunate accident, and I'd like to put it behind us."

Justin nodded and shook the older man's hand. "Agreed. Justin Marchan. Starting over makes sense." He relaxed his shoulders. "We plan to live here a long time, and we don't want to be at war with our neighbors."

Kristin stepped up and reached out to shake Marcus' hand too. "I'm Kristin Marchan. Your wife is lovely, and I look forward to getting to know both of you better."

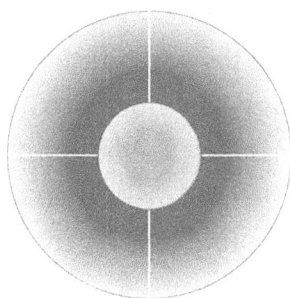

Chapter Three

As the weeks passed, Kristin threw herself into planning her new business with renewed energy. She felt motivated in a way she hadn't in years, as if someone had lifted a veil from her eyes. She'd spent hours researching local zoning regulations, reading up on animal behavior, and sketching out designs for the dog daycare facility. It was work, but it didn't feel like a burden. It felt like purpose.

True to his word, Benjamin Pike stayed in touch. They met once a week, sometimes over coffee, other times during long walks at the nature preserve. He asked questions more than he gave advice, subtly steering her toward her own conclusions. His presence became a steady influence—part mentor, part friend, part confessor.

One breezy afternoon, they sat on a shaded bench on the greenway trail off the community golf course. Kristin was flipping through her notebook, talking about the contractor she wanted to hire to build the outdoor play area for the dogs. Ben listened, then asked, "And what about the people around you? What do they think of your plans?"

Kristin hesitated. "You mean the neighbors? I guess I haven't really thought about it. We got off to a rough start with one neighbor, but that all died down. I've been so focused on getting it up and running, I had no time to talk to anyone else."

Ben nodded. "I think you might want to consider the community circle. Sometimes it's the most overlooked. And yet, it's the one that can make or break our progress."

"I never thought about that. So, you think I should talk to them?"

"It's not just about courtesy. It's about connection. Trust me, Kristin. You want to be seen as a good neighbor, not just someone who puts up a fence and does her own thing."

"I guess it can't hurt. So far, we only know one neighbor, and they're quite a bit older, so I'm not sure what we have in common. The other houses around us are filled with DINKs."

Ben tilted his head. "Dinks? You'll have to explain."

Kristin laughed. "Double income, no kids." Then,

a pensive look crossed her face. "It's actually kind of lonely. They all leave early in the morning and don't get home until early evening. I guess that's good for me though. They won't be around during the day when I have the dogs here."

"Perhaps, but that doesn't mean they don't care or won't know what you're doing. It's up to you."

That evening, Kristin brought the idea up to Justin over dinner. He raised an eyebrow at first but agreed. "If this business is going to be part of our lives," he said, "maybe it should be part of the neighborhood, too. If they have a problem, better we know about it now."

The next weekend, Kristin invited Marcus and Pamela Stephens along with three other close by neighbors over for coffee and scones on the deck. After the usual chit-chat and introductions, Kristin started talking about her idea. It was informal, and she used it as a chance to share her vision and hear their concerns. There was very little response, positive or negative.

In an effort to make peace, Pamela spoke up. "Kristin and I are becoming good friends, and Marcus and I support this venture of hers. We love enterprising young people." She turned to Kristin. "But I have to warn you. You can expect a call from Marcus about the insurance you'll need for your business."

That broke the tension, and everyone laughed. The group asked lots of questions about noise and traffic, and Kristin did her best to assure them she was already working on solutions. Her openness impressed them, and to her and Justin's relief, in the end, they were very supportive. One neighbor even offered to introduce her to someone who ran a successful boarding kennel near Danbury.

After they left, Kristin felt lighter. She texted Ben: Had the neighbors over. It went well. You were right—again.

He replied a few minutes later: You did the hard part. Keep going.

It was a small victory, but one that made a big difference. Kristin was no longer just starting a business. She was building something much deeper: a life connected to others, driven by passion, and guided by wisdom from someone who understood what a well-lived life really looked like.

⦿⦿⦿⦿

Marcus didn't attend the neighborhood gathering at the Marchan's. He was fighting his own frustrations. His insurance agency wasn't performing like it used to. Leads had slowed, and his attempts to revive sales felt stale. Even renewals were dropping. Instead, he went to the office that day to review his book of business and try to come up with a plan.

Two hours later, he was more discouraged than when he started. He looked at the picture of he and Pamela on his desk. He and Pamela had their picture taken ten years ago while vacationing in Hawaii. The tanned faces and beaming smiles reminded him of happier times. Recently, he and Pamela seemed out of sync, often letting minor disagreements grow larger than necessary.

Marcus decided to call Ben. "Hey, my friend. Long time, no talk. Do you have a few minutes to talk?"

"I've always got time for you. Why don't you drive up to the orchard? I'll bribe you with my best pressed cider."

"I'll be there in forty-5 minutes." Marcus hung up and drove to Pound Ridge.

They settled on the back porch with tall glasses of Ben's ice-cold cider. "Now, tell me what's on your mind."

Marcus poured out his worries—financial uncertainty, pressure at work, and tension at home.

Ben nodded slowly. "You're trying to control outcomes," he said. "But maybe the invitation here is to re-center. Look at your 5 circles. Which ones are being neglected?"

That question hit Marcus hard. He realized he'd been so focused on finances that he'd let his spiritual, family, community, and personal life drift.

Ben encouraged him to make room—not just for strategy, but for vision. "Lead with values," Ben said. "People follow that. Even in business. As for Pam, when was the last time you brought her flowers?"

Marcus went home with more clarity than he'd had in weeks. The bouquet of seasonal flowers sat on the coffee table in Pamela's favorite vase. After dinner, they sat down and started a real conversation. Not about spreadsheets or stress, but about what they each wanted for their future.

"I thought by now we'd be on easy-street, looking at a comfortable retirement," Marcus said.

"We're not destitute. We've been through these ups-and-downs before. I'm not worried, honey. I have faith in you." Pamela was always the voice of reason.

"I wish I shared that faith, Pam. I feel like I'm failing you."

"Oh, pish posh. In all the years we've been married, you've never failed me. We'll figure this out. Why don't you make an appointment to see Jeremy? He's never given us bad advice, and maybe he'll have some ideas."

"I'm not sure our financial advisor is what I need right now. What I need is a miracle."

⭕⭕⭕⭕

Midtown Manhattan throbbed with its usual chaos—honking horns, jaywalking pedestrians, cabbies weaving through lanes like stunt drivers—but Marcus barely registered it anymore. Trapped in his Mercedes, inching forward beneath another stubborn red light, he regretted not taking the train. He wasn't just late—he was anxious. The upcoming meeting had been looming in his mind all week, a pit of dread that no amount of leather seating or climate control could soothe.

Even the soothing tones of classical music, piped in through the car's sound system, failed to calm the financial storm stirring inside him. He toggled it off midway through a Mozart concerto, letting the ambient drone of the city wash over him as he climbed the ramps of the garage adjacent to the gleaming skyscraper.

Marcus had been in tighter financial spots before, but not with so much at stake. His insurance brokerage, once a stable operation, had been squeezed by industry disruption, shifting customer habits, and relentless competition. COVID had only accelerated what felt like a tectonic shift. And now, years of aggressive investing and forced cash withdrawals were converging in a way he could no longer ignore.

Inside the lobby of Jeremy Watkins and Associates, Marcus was momentarily distracted by the receptionist—a stunning young woman with the kind of poise his friend always seemed to surround himself with. Jeremy, after all, had always been a man of good taste and sharper instincts. Even in college, while Marcus chased early sales leads and partied with fraternity brothers, Jeremy had been poring over investment textbooks alone on Friday nights.

"Do you have an appointment, sir?" the receptionist asked, her tone polished and polite.

"Old Marcus here is welcome anytime," Jeremy announced, striding into the lobby with a confident grin.

The banter was welcome, even familiar, but Marcus's smile was forced. Jeremy's office—polished oak, floor-to-ceiling windows, skyline views—was a testament to success. And that success stood in stark contrast to the numbers Marcus had been dreading.

The conversation turned quickly, as it always did with Jeremy, from pleasantries to reality. Marcus appreciated that about him. No sugarcoating. No flattery. Just the truth—whether he was ready or not.

"You've been putting your foot on the accelerator way too much," Jeremy said, laying a spreadsheet flat on his desk. "You're down thirty percent, Marcus. That's not a dip—that's a crater."

Marcus's throat tightened. He knew it was bad. But he didn't expect confirmation of just how deeply his financial future had eroded.

The truth was simple and brutal. He had ignored Jeremy's advice and gambled on flashy tech stocks, convinced he could outmaneuver the market. He'd pulled money at the worst times, drained funds to cover business expenses when his brokerage's cash flow dipped, and justified every decision hoping things would rebound soon.

But the rebound never came.

"I had to make those withdrawals," he said, his tone defensive but also weary. "The company needed the cash. Competition's cutthroat now. The old playbook doesn't work anymore."

Jeremy understood, but he wasn't going to pretend that reality was softer than it was. "Maybe so," he said. "But you're chasing retirement with a broken leg."

Marcus had been clinging to the idea of retiring in three years. It was his light at the end of the tunnel, the dream that gave meaning to the grueling days. He envisioned time with his wife, his grandkids, maybe even the legacy of leaving his brokerage in good shape to a new buyer, since his son had his own career and no interest in insurance. But Jeremy's words flattened that dream under a new timeline—5 years, likely more.

To salvage his plans, Marcus would need a hard pivot. That meant scaling up the brokerage quickly— bringing in new accounts, expanding his client base, and reducing risky exposure. The business would need not just to survive but to thrive. And with industry headwinds and no staff, that was far from guaranteed.

Still, Jeremy's strategy gave Marcus a thread to hold

on to: shift to index funds, rein in the risk, build value in the brokerage, and stretch the runway.

He nodded slowly, the weight of the conversation settling in his chest. "I've been thinking the same thing. It's just hard when you feel like you're sprinting uphill while the ground gives way beneath you."

He shared the recent episode with the neighbor's dogs—his anger, his outburst—symptomatic of a deeper unease. His fuse was shorter now, and he recognized it wasn't just about neighborhood boundaries. It was about control—control he felt slipping not just from his finances, but from his identity as a provider, a professional, a patriarch.

"I want to leave something behind," he confessed. "Not just for Pam and me—but for my son, for the grandkids. I lie awake thinking about that legacy."

Jeremy offered him a lifeline in the form of friendship. "Let's make a date for tennis soon," he said. "Start keeping your body young while we work on your balance sheet."

Marcus smiled, but behind it was a man sobered by consequence. The future he envisioned wasn't gone— but it would take grit, strategy, and humility to reach it.

He stood, shook Jeremy's hand, and accepted the invitation. "Maybe I'll even win this time," he said.

Jeremy's laugh was warm. "Highly doubtful."

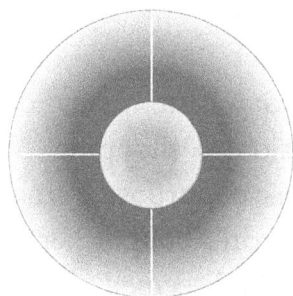

Chapter Four

With their 33rd wedding anniversary just around the corner, Marcus Stephens found himself reflecting more often than usual. Gratitude came easily to him these days—gratitude for Pamela, for their family, for the life they'd built together. It wasn't perfect, of course—whose life was—but Marcus wasn't one to dwell on the flaws. He'd long since adopted the belief that love wasn't about grand gestures or flawless days, but about loyalty, partnership, and endurance.

Still, he wanted to do something special this year—something that went beyond flowers or a dinner reservation. He wasn't the sentimental type, not outwardly, and writing things like "I love you more today than on our wedding day" in a card felt too corny for his taste. But a gift . . . the right gift . . . might say it for him.

So, on Saturday afternoon, despite his well-documented aversion to shopping, Marcus headed to the mall with a sense of purpose. Pamela had mentioned recently that she hadn't bought herself new clothes in quite a while. That had seemed like a good lead—until he walked into two high-end boutiques and realized just how out of his depth he was. He knew her size, yes, but fashion? He had as much chance of picking the right blouse as he did guessing her favorite perfume blindfolded.

In the end, he made the safe bet: jewelry. It had never failed him before.

The jewelry store clerk, a young woman with a warm smile and an eye for husbands on a mission, patiently guided him. Together, they chose a delicate gold heart-shaped pendant necklace. He had their wedding date engraved on it—a small, elegant symbol of the life they'd lived side by side.

While the engraving was being done, Marcus wandered into the bookstore. The Civil War section caught his eye, as always. He'd long been fascinated by history—not just the battles and timelines, but the human grit behind them. He picked up a new book on the Battle of Antietam, appreciating the weight of it in his hands. A quiet gift to himself.

As he drove home with the wrapped necklace resting on the passenger seat, his thoughts drifted back to the conversation he'd had with Jeremy earlier that week. Early retirement was no longer on the horizon. The numbers didn't lie. But he didn't want to bring any of that up just yet. This weekend was about Pamela.

Just Pamela.

⬭⬭⬭⬭

Sunday morning arrived with the soft scent of sizzling bacon floating through the house. Marcus blinked awake to find Pamela already gone from bed. The morning light filtered through the open blinds, and the house felt warm in a way that had nothing to do with the weather.

Still in his robe and slippers, he made his way downstairs. Pamela stood in the kitchen, humming softly over a pan of bacon, dressed in a bright floral sundress with an apron tied neatly around her waist. She turned, smiled, and greeted him with a kiss that lingered.

"Happy anniversary," she said.

The day unfolded in quiet harmony. They exchanged cards and gifts. Pamela was delighted by the necklace and fastened it around her neck with a glow that Marcus would remember for a long time. Her gift to him—a pair of 50-yard-line tickets to a Giants game—made his eyes widen with joy. It wasn't just the gift itself; it was how well she knew him.

That evening, they drove to Westport for dinner at Zino's, a bistro known for its authentic Northern Italian cuisine. It brought back memories of a ski trip to the Italian Alps decades ago, when they'd first fallen in love with that style of food—and with each other. They sat in a quiet corner, a bay window framing Long Island Sound beyond the candlelit table. Their laughter came easily, warmed by wine and nostalgia.

As it always did on their anniversary, the conversation drifted back in time. To college. To the first time they met. Marcus remembered every detail—how Pamela had been dating one of his friends during freshman year, and how, the moment they broke up, he wasted no time calling her.

"You didn't even give me 5 minutes to get over it," she teased.

"I knew I had to move fast," he said, "before someone else got to you."

She laughed, leaning into his shoulder. It was a memory worn soft with age, but no less cherished.

After dinner, they took a slow walk along the marina. The docks were quiet, the night warm, the water lapping gently against the hulls of anchored yachts.

Marcus admired a sleek cabin cruiser with a fiberglass hull that gleamed under the dock lights. "Think it's too late for me to own one of these?" he asked. "By the time I retire, I might not be able to hoist a sail."

He was only half-joking. Boats had always symbolized something more to him—freedom, escape, a reward for a life of hard work. But practicality and responsibility had kept that dream just out of reach.

Pamela pulled him toward a bench, sensing the deeper worry beneath his words. "Why are you talking like you're an old man? You're still in great shape," she said, touching his arm playfully.

Marcus smiled, but the cloud hadn't quite lifted. "I know we said we wouldn't talk money this weekend, but I have to be honest, Pam—the next few years are critical. They'll decide whether we retire comfortably or just get by."

Pamela didn't flinch. She'd been waiting for this opening.

"Well," she said carefully, "you told Jeremy the key is building up your business so it's attractive to buyers, right?"

He looked at her, knowing her well enough to sense what was coming. "That's a big part of it, yes."

"I think I can help with that," she said. "I want to go back to work at the agency."

Marcus blinked. It wasn't something he'd expected to hear tonight, of all nights—but maybe he should have. Their whole journey had been marked by shared effort.

When she'd become pregnant in college, she gave up her degree. When he took over the agency, she earned her license and supported him while raising Greg. And later, she gave up even that to care for the grandkids when Greg and his wife needed help.

"You don't have to do that," he said. "You love spending time with Sammy and Suzy. And it'll throw off the kids' routine if you're not available to babysit."

"They're smart. They'll figure it out," she replied. "We need to think about us now. With me back at the agency, we can free up enough money to make our dreams possible."

"What about Charles?" Marcus asked. The young employee he mentored was bright and eager—but in a small office, someone would have to go.

"He'll land on his feet," Pamela said gently. "He's got a bright future. But we've sacrificed long enough. It's our turn now."

Marcus hesitated. "Do you really want to go back to the grind?"

"Honestly? No," she admitted. "But I know that job inside and out. I could do it four days a week, taking Wednesdays off for errands. It's manageable." He looked at her with fresh admiration. "You've thought this through."

"I have," she nodded. "This isn't just your retirement, Marcus. It's ours. And we're a team, remember?"

He took her hand and sighed. "So, you're saying it's time we put ourselves first?"

She smiled. "That's not selfish. That's overdue."

He chuckled softly. "I've been reading so many articles about retirement planning lately, I should've seen this coming. I'm just stubborn."

"You always are," she said, leaning in for a kiss. "But I love you anyway."

They stood together, watching the moonlight shimmer across the boats. Hope and resolve bloomed between them, a reminder that the next few years wasn't about endings, but about new beginnings—this time, on their terms.

"Thanks for making this such a great anniversary," she said.

Marcus looked at the cruiser one more time and smiled. "With even better ones to come."

"That's the spirit, Captain."

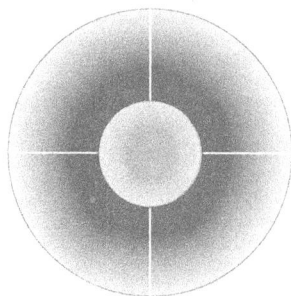

Chapter Five

By early September, Kristin's dream was no longer a vague ambition—it was a developing reality. Construction on the kennels had begun, and the backyard was a buzz of activity. Workers came and went, measuring, cutting, hauling, and assembling under the late summer sun. Kristin managed it all with a quiet confidence that surprised even herself. Justin, who had once been skeptical, was beginning to admire her resolve.

Marcus and Pamela Stephens watched with a mix of curiosity and concern. Marcus, being the insurance guy, appreciated structure and predictability. But lately, there had been a lot of barking. A lot of cars and trucks. A lot of disruption. Not at all what Kristin promised.

Pamela, on the other hand, was more intrigued than

annoyed. She admired Kristin's energy. One day, after running into her at the grocery store, she told Marcus, "She's not just building a business. She's building something with heart."

"Heart doesn't keep property values up," Marcus muttered, though not harshly. "Still, maybe we should talk to them again. Get a better sense of what's going on."

That chance came sooner than expected. Kristin invited a few neighbors over for a second informal gathering—this time more like a community forum. She shared detailed drawings of the planned facilities. Kristin didn't sugarcoat anything. She addressed concerns about barking and traffic head-on, explaining her plans for soundproofing, staggered pickup times, and a dedicated access path off the main road.

Despite the concerns raised, even Marcus came around. He appreciated her transparency and organization.

"She's not winging it," he told Pamela afterward. "She's thought it all through."

Pamela smiled. "Sounds like someone I know."

As Kristin's project gained momentum, so did her friendship with Pamela. They chatted frequently— on neighborhood walks, over coffee, and eventually, confiding in each other. Pamela shared that she was rejoining the family insurance business to help Marcus get things back on track. "It's been a challenge," she admitted. "But maybe a good one."

Kristin nodded. "Ben would say it's about balance. About the 5 circles."

Pamela raised an eyebrow. "I forgot you were talking to Benjamin Pike. Sounds like he's got another fan. Marcus and I have been friends with him for years. But I must say, we're not so good at following through on all his sage advice."

"I find him to be charming and insightful. Sort of like a lighthouse in a fog."

"What a great way to describe him. He is one of a kind. I have never met such a generous man," Pamela said.

"I think I finally convinced Justin to meet with Ben. There is something going on with him, and I can't put my finger on it."

The following week, Kristin invited Ben to meet her and Justin for lunch.

They met at a quiet bistro downtown. Over sandwiches and iced tea, Benjamin listened more than he spoke, his calm demeanor setting the tone. When the conversation turned to long-term goals, he gently challenged Justin. "We've spent so much time talking about Kristin's plans that I haven't heard enough about you. What is it that you want to do—and not just that, but who do you want to become?"

Justin shrugged. "I've been thinking about that more than I expected. And to be honest, I'm not sure I like who I've been lately."

Kristin shot him a quizzical look.

Ben nodded. "Then maybe it's time to reimagine your definition of success."

"I've always been focused on the money. Listening to you and Kristin, I'm beginning to realize maybe there's a lot more to life."

Kristin put her hand over Justin's. "You know I don't care about the money. I want you to be happy. I want us to be happy."

"Are you saying you're not happy?" Justin's voice betrayed his anxiety.

"No, of course not. I'm not saying it right. Ben got me thinking about the bigger picture, about the future, about the parts of our lives that we don't seem to focus on."

Priorities were shifting for Kristin and Justin, but Ben sensed there was something going on that Justin wasn't sharing. He knew the best role for him to play was to remain somewhere in the background, and hopefully guide them to seek a life not just of achievement, but of true abundance.

Kristin had entered college in New Haven with the vague conviction that biology held the key to her future. Like many young students, she wavered between dreams and doubts—veterinary school had once seemed like the path, but the rigor of certain courses and her own quiet insecurities wore away at that ambition. She wasn't sure where she belonged, and each semester made that uncertainty feel a little more permanent.

Money was tight. Her parents helped where they could, encouraging her to take on student loans to fill the gap. But Kristin, practical and proud, resisted the idea of starting adult life burdened by debt. Instead, she took on part-time work as a cashier at a local coffee shop, trading study hours for shifts and late nights on her feet.

That's where she met Justin.

He came in like clockwork, always ordering a mocha latte and a croissant, always armed with some absurd joke or awkward pun. His humor was harmlessly relentless—designed not just to amuse, but to charm. He was a Yale student, strikingly handsome, but more disarming than he was arrogant. In time, the girl with the worn biology textbook and the boy with the bad jokes became something more. Not long after graduation, they were married.

Their first year together in a small New York City apartment was a blur of noise, spontaneity, and youthful energy. They lived modestly, with the wide-eyed wonder of newlyweds who had little but needed nothing. Until everything changed.

Justin's grandfather, a towering figure in his life, died unexpectedly of a heart attack. The emotional blow ran deep; they had been close in a way that surpassed the usual generational bond. His passing left Justin grieving—but also suddenly, inexplicably, wealthy. The man who had always treated Justin as his heir, not just in name but in spirit, had left him a $15 million trust fund.

The inheritance changed the couple's life overnight. With careful guidance and no shortage of surprise, they stepped into a new tax bracket—and into a world they had never envisioned for themselves. A six-million-dollar home in New Canaan on 5 luscious acres, complete with manicured grounds and mature trees, became their new reality.

Kristin sometimes wondered if that tiny coffee shop version of herself—struggling, uncertain, hopeful—would recognize the life she now lived. And while neither she nor Justin wore their wealth loudly, both knew it had altered the terrain of their marriage, their decisions, and their future.

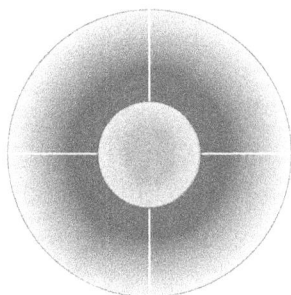

Chapter Six

A fter meeting with Jeremy, Marcus tackled his efforts to grow the insurance agency with renewed energy, even cautious optimism. Having Pamela back working with him gave him a much-needed boost. He believed that by bolstering revenues and expanding the client base, he could push the business to a point where it would fetch a strong valuation—enough to support his long-held retirement goals. But as the weeks passed, his confidence began to erode. Despite his best intentions and well-rehearsed pitches, results lagged. He brought in some new clients, yes, but nowhere near enough to offset the attrition or match the targets he'd set.

He'd been in sales long enough to know where the line between persistence and pushiness lay, and he respected it. But lately, that respect felt like a handicap. Meeting after meeting ended with the same canned phrases: "I'll have to think about it," "I'm weighing my options," "Let's put a pin in this for now." Each time, Marcus smiled politely, masking the sting. Behind closed doors, though, frustration simmered. People made six-figure decisions about houses in a heartbeat—but ask them to commit to a policy that could protect their family's future, and suddenly the brakes were slammed on.

Worse than the lack of conversions were the cancellations. Longtime clients were either downsizing or defecting to cheaper competitors. He couldn't blame them—uncertainty clung to the economy like fog. Still, each loss chipped away at the foundation he'd spent decades building. With every dropped policy, Marcus stared out his office window longer, watching clouds drift and wondering—What if I just sold now? Walked away? He knew it wasn't practical. The market wasn't right, the agency wasn't strong enough yet, and such a move would kill his retirement strategy. But the temptation offered a strange kind of relief. Just thinking about quitting helped him endure another day.

Then came the call from Jeremy.

It was a scheduled update—nothing out of the ordinary—but Marcus could tell by the tone it wasn't good news. Detrimental shifts in the market. Some of his investments had taken a hit. Not catastrophic, but enough to keep his stomach in knots and aspirin bottle half-empty for the afternoon.

He didn't complain much—not out loud. Not to colleagues, not to friends. But Pamela, his wife, bore the weight of it secondhand. They were bickering more often now. Little comments ignited big sparks. He couldn't talk to her the way he once did. She had always been a calm, steady presence in his life, but lately, she seemed brittle, as though any small pressure might shatter her composure. Maybe having her come back to work wasn't a good idea.

He recalled a moment from just a few days earlier. He'd casually mentioned how long it had been since they had seen the kids. Her reaction was swift, sharp. "You think I don't want to? I'm too busy! I can't do everything!" The edge in her voice startled him.

He decided he'd try again today. It was Wednesday— her day off. Maybe with a little rest she'd be in a better mood. Maybe he could tell her about Jeremy's report, about the portfolio, about how exhausted he felt just trying to keep the business afloat.

But when he stepped into the house, something felt wrong.

It was too quiet. No TV. No music. Just stillness.

Then came the sound. Muffled, low, but unmistakable—crying. Deep sobbing. He followed it to the bedroom, and there she was—curled in a fetal position on their king-sized bed, wearing old sweats and a tattered T-shirt he hadn't seen in years.

"Pam!" He was beside her in seconds, lifting her gently into his arms. "What happened? What's wrong?"

She didn't answer. She just wept against his shoulder.

He held her, resisting the urge to fill the silence with questions. Eventually, the trembling subsided. She excused herself to the bathroom, dried her face, and returned with puffy eyes and a voice barely holding steady.

"I just came back from the doctor," she said. "I have cancer."

The word struck like a hammer. In that moment, Marcus's thoughts splintered. Friends, relatives—he'd seen what cancer could do. But Pamela? The notion was unbearable.

He stammered. "Oh God." Then the questions rushed out—What kind? How far along? Is it treatable?

She answered with a composure that stunned him. "Breast cancer. They caught it early. They say the prognosis is good if I start aggressive treatment."

She tried to stay strong. He tried to stay upright. Neither quite managed it.

Dinner plans evaporated. She insisted he go out, get something simple. "I need some space, and so do you." He didn't want to leave her, but part of him understood. Sometimes when life caves in, solitude becomes a refuge.

He found himself at the golf club bar, pushing through a cheeseburger and nursing a beer while pretending to watch a baseball game he didn't care about. The place was nearly empty. The kind of quiet that made it feel like the world had stopped spinning.

Then, out of the corner of his eye, he saw someone.

Justin Marchan.

His neighbor. The man he'd argued with and never really warmed to.

Marcus almost turned away. But something compelled him to slide down the bar and take the seat next to him.

"Small world, huh?" he said, voice neutral.

Justin looked up slowly. "Oh, it's you, Stephens." He offered a tentative handshake.

Marcus took it. The tension between them seemed to ease.

Justin asked, "Did you just finish a game?"

"No. Just needed to get out of the house. Got some bad news."

Justin nodded solemnly. "Me too."

There was a quiet honesty in the moment, an unspoken understanding. Marcus hesitated, then spoke.

"My wife has cancer."

Justin's expression shifted instantly. Concern over

-took the haze in his eyes. "Damn. I'm so sorry to hear that. My aunt's a survivor—Sloan-Kettering saved her life. If you ever need anything—"

"Thanks," Marcus said. "She's got good doctors. But I appreciate it."

The conversation shifted subtly. Justin began to open up. As it turned out, he wasn't just here to unwind—he was unraveling.

He admitted to a drinking problem. One that had cost him his job. Worse, he'd burned through much of his trust fund—money he never expected to lose.

Marcus asked quietly, "How's Kristin handling it?"

Justin stared at his glass. "She doesn't know. I haven't told her."

They sat in silence, the kind that holds more than words ever could.

Then a third voice broke in. "What brings you here, Ben?"

It was Benjamin Pike, still in golf clothes, cheerful and composed.

"Even at my age, there's room for improvement," he said with a grin. Then, noticing the grim looks on their faces, he added, "Everything alright?"

Justin shook his head and pushed his scotch away. "I'm unemployed."

Marcus followed, his voice thick with emotion. "It's Pam. She has cancer."

Ben's smile evaporated. He pulled up a stool and rested his arms on the bar.

"These kinds of crises," he said, "and believe me, I know; they touch every part of your life. It all gets hit at once."

Justin looked skeptical. "Yeah. So what?"

"So," Ben continued, "knowing that is the first step. If you can identify where it's hurting, you can start healing. Let's get a table and have a talk."

Ben ordered coffee for everyone and listened as Justin and Marcus filled in a few more details. After a time, he shared his own story about loss. He told them about how he and Margaret almost lost their house because of medical bills, and how empty he felt after she died. The pain in his voice was real, but so was the wisdom.

"I know my problems are not your problems. I only share because I want you to know there is always light at the end of the tunnel. Sometimes, you need a fresh set of batteries in your flashlight so you can see the way."

Justin and Marcus shook their heads, but neither spoke. Ben continued. "By facing each part of my life— one at a time—I found a way through. Not around. Through."

He turned the conversation back to the men. "Marcus, from what you said, Pam's prognosis is good." Marcus nodded. "And Justin, you're young and smart and healthy. Don't let short-term setbacks keep you from moving forward." Justin stared into his coffee cup.

The bar was empty. But for the first time all day, Marcus didn't feel alone, and neither did Justin. The men sat in silence as they drained their cups.

And somehow, against all odds, there was the faintest flicker of hope.

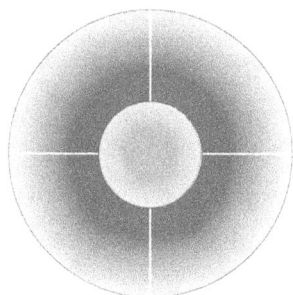

Chapter Seven

Justin Marchan had not been honest with Kristin—not about his job, or more accurately, the absence of one. Fired days ago, he still hadn't found the courage to tell her. He clung to the excuse that he needed time to "clear his head," but what he was really doing was hiding—from her, from reality, and from the image of himself he could no longer uphold.

As his nearly new Mercedes glided through late-morning traffic, heading north away from New Canaan rather than toward Manhattan, Justin kept his eyes fixed on the road, but his thoughts were unraveling. He needed somewhere familiar, somewhere with memories unmarred by failure. So, he chose Yale. His alma mater. A place where life had once felt limitless.

He parked in a downtown garage and walked the campus, ignoring everyone he passed, seeing only the trimmed hedges and stone buildings whispering of better days. On the far edge of a green lawn, he found the gazebo where he and Kristin had shared their first kiss beneath a moonlit sky. Now, seated on a weathered bench nearby, he took a long breath and tried to sort through the wreckage of his life.

The truth was harsh. Inheriting fifteen million dollars should have been a blessing, but it had unmoored him. For all his financial savvy, he had spent recklessly—not out of greed, but ego. He wanted to impress, to prove something. Luxury cars, exotic vacations, speculative investments made under pressure from friends, and yes, a six-million-dollar home—it all seemed justified at the time. It wasn't. And when things began to spiral, he didn't confide in Kristin. Not because he feared her worry, but because he feared her judgment. Confessing the truth meant exposing his deepest insecurity: that he was not, in fact, the invincible, self-made success he pretended to be.

Worse, to dull the stress, Justin had turned to alcohol. A lunchtime drink became two, then three. He drank after work. He drank on weekends. When Kristin finally confronted him, he'd waved it off, insisting he didn't have "a problem." But he did.

As he rose from the bench, he passed a young couple

laughing together beneath a tree-lined walkway. The image twisted something inside him. Once, that had been him and Kristin. Now, he was returning home to shatter her trust. He couldn't avoid it any longer.

It was early afternoon when he finally arrived. Kristin, as expected, was in the backyard training area, working with the dogs alongside Stan, the retired pet store owner she'd hired to assist her. Roxi, a lively English Shepherd, bounded through a tunnel and earned a treat and praise from Kristin. But when she spotted Justin, something in his posture signaled that something was wrong.

She jogged over and kissed him. "Hi, honey. Everything okay?"

He hesitated. "Well, I, um . . ."

She saw it instantly—his struggle. She turned to Stan. "Can you take over for a bit while I talk to Justin?"

Inside the kitchen, the air was cool. Beads of sweat evaporated from Kristin's forehead as she sat across from Justin and took his hand. "Something's wrong. I can feel it. What is it—something at the office?"

Justin exhaled. "There's no easy way to say this . . . I've been let go."

He watched her face for a reaction and saw a rapid shift—shock, confusion, hurt.

"What?" she asked, barely containing her disbelief. "Was this some kind of downsizing? When did this happen?"

"A few days ago," he admitted.

She pulled her hand away. Her eyes, wide with disbelief, narrowed in frustration. "And you're just telling me now?"

"I knew you'd react like this," he shot back defensively.

"Well, how should I react? We promised—no secrets!"

"I was trying to protect you!" The old lie came too easily.

"I'm not a child," she snapped. "We're a team—or we're supposed to be."

Her tone softened. "Please. Tell me the whole story. Don't leave anything out."

Shaken, Justin finally laid it all bare—his job loss, his drinking, the financial spiral. He told her everything.

Kristin listened, but her composure cracked. She stood up. "I need time," she said, heading for the door.

He sat frozen, humiliated. "So that's it? The silent treatment?"

She stopped at the door. "I just need to get some air. We'll talk later."

And with that, she was gone.

Kristin walked quickly, directionless but unable to slow down. Her mind raced: How could he do this? She felt betrayed. Misled. Still, beneath the anger, a quiet longing stirred—the desire to help him—to salvage what could still be saved.

Without realizing it, she had walked to the Stephens' driveway. Pamela's white SUV was parked outside. Kristin hesitated. Pamela was older, more of a maternal figure than a peer. But they had grown close. And Kristin needed someone—now.

She stepped through the gate and found Pamela lying on a lounge chair by the pool, wrapped in a pink robe, her hair undone, eyes red and puffy.

"Hi," Pamela said weakly.

Kristin sat beside her without hesitation. Thoughts of Justin momentarily vanished. "Are you okay? You don't look like yourself."

Pamela adjusted the lounge upright and tried to compose herself. "Just a little health scare."

Kristin nodded sympathetically. "I don't want to pry, but I just had a very hard conversation with someone I love who's been keeping things in. And let me tell you, it doesn't help." She placed a hand gently on Pamela's arm. "Are you sure there's not something you want to share?"

That was all it took. Pamela told her everything—the breast cancer diagnosis, the fear, the uncertainty.

"I'm terrified," she admitted. "They say the prognosis is good, but I've heard the stories. The treatments . . . I don't know if I can handle it."

Kristin pulled her into a hug. "You're strong, Pamela. I've seen it. And if anyone can beat this, it's you."

For the first time that day, Pamela smiled.

They talked more. Pamela confessed she felt guilty for getting sick just when Marcus needed her most.

Kristin sighed. "At least Marcus keeps you in the loop. Justin didn't even tell me he lost his job."

Now it was Pamela's turn to listen.

Kristin shared the details of the confrontation, her frustration, and—despite it all—her desire to help. "Yes, he messed up," she said. "But he's my husband. I just want to help him find a way forward."

Pamela perked up. "Funny you say that. Marcus is inside right now talking with Ben Pike."

Kristin smiled. "I love Ben. He's brilliant."

Without another word, Kristin pulled out her phone and texted Justin: Sorry for walking out. Please meet me across the street. There's someone here we should talk to. Love you. 😊

Ten minutes later, the Marchans and the Stephens sat in the spacious living room, each couple on their own sofa. Between them sat Benjamin Pike, grounded and serene in a high-backed recliner.

He listened carefully, then spoke. "The hardest part is done—you've recognized what matters. These arguments, these divisions? They're small things.

Setbacks put life in perspective. And they remind us how much we have in common."

The couples nodded. The tension had already begun to lift.

Ben leaned forward. "Now it's time to stop looking back and start planning forward. Set your goals. Large and small. Look at your relationships—yourself, your faith, your families, your community, your finances. They're all connected."

"But what about the things we can't control, like Pam's breast cancer?" Marcus pressed his hands together until his knuckles turned white.

Ben nodded. "You have more control than you think. You have options. You have choices to make. From what Pam told me, there is every reason to be hopeful."

Pam nodded. "Ben's right. My doctor said this is not a death sentence; just a setback."

Marcus was not convinced. "You always talk about 'the abundant life.' What does that really mean?"

"Great question," Ben replied. "It's not about wealth or comfort. It's about how you respond to adversity. You can let setbacks destroy you—or you can let them refine you."

He looked around the room, making eye contact with each of them.

"So let me ask you," he said quietly, "as individuals, as couples—what does abundance look like... to you?"

The room fell into thoughtful silence.

But something had changed—not just in circumstance, but in spirit. The healing had started.

$$\infty\infty\infty$$

By mid-September, the days were growing shorter and the evenings cooler, but the energy in the neighborhood was just beginning to warm.

Justin enrolled in law school at Yale, committed to putting his energy into shaping a new career. Their remaining inheritance covered the first-year's tuition and gave him the much-needed breathing room to get his life back on track. He kept a chart of the 5 circles in the front of his notebook and made a point of looking at them every day to make sure he was giving space to each one.

Kristin's dog care center was taking shape rapidly, and the carefully orchestrated plans to minimize neighborhood disruption were proving effective. Pamela referred to it as "the boutique kennel," admiring how Kristin managed to blend professionalism with warmth.

Yet it wasn't just Kristin's project that was evolving. The relationships between the neighbors were, too. And at the center of this slow transformation was Benjamin Pike.

It was Ben who suggested the idea for a Trivia Night fundraiser at the church—something lighthearted, but with purpose. "It'll be good for the congregation," he told the pastor. "People are eager for connection, especially when so many are facing transitions."

He was right.

Kristin and Justin volunteered to help with the event, and so did Marcus and Pamela. The four found themselves spending more time together, and even Marcus admitted that Justin was no longer that flashy city guy. He was smart, and funny, and surprisingly humble when he let his guard down.

On the night of the event, the church's newly constructed youth center was packed. Kristin and Marcus ended up on the same team, and their combination of pop culture knowledge and historical trivia made them surprisingly formidable.

During a break between rounds, Benjamin took the mic and offered a short reflection. "Tonight isn't just about raising money," he said. "It's about remembering who we are as a community. Whether you're a lifelong member or just moved in, whether you're starting something new or looking to find your footing again—this is your circle."

He made eye contact with Marcus, then Kristin, and finally Pamela and Justin.

Later that night, after their team had claimed victory with a dramatic final-round answer, they all stayed to help clean up. Marcus found himself walking with Ben, carrying trash bags out to the dumpster.

"You always know what to say," Marcus said.

Ben chuckled. "Not always. But I try to listen more than I talk. People usually tell you what they need—if you let them."

As they returned to the building, Ben added, "Marcus, can I give you one piece of advice?"

"Sure."

"Don't wait for the perfect time to make a change. If your business is struggling, if you're not sleeping at night, don't white-knuckle your way through it. Ask for help. Talk to your wife. Bring your team into the vision. That's how you build a legacy."

Marcus nodded. He didn't say anything right away. But the words sat with him.

⬭⬭⬭⬭

Storm clouds were gathering on the horizon. Complaints soon emerged in the neighborhood. Increased traffic from dog owners and the sounds of barking began to ruffle feathers. Caught between their neighbors' expectations and their friendship with the Marchans, Pamela and Marcus found themselves in a tough spot.

One evening, Pamela walked across the street and found Kristin training a group of puppies in the yard.

She waited until the session was over, then invited her inside for tea.

"I think we need to talk," Pamela said gently.

Kristin's face fell. "I've heard. The cars. The noise. I didn't mean for it to be a problem. I've just been working extra hard and taking on more dogs. You know, with Justin in school, I feel even more pressure for this business to succeed."

Pamela reassured her. "You're doing something special. But maybe now's the time to connect even more with the community—not just with clients, but also with your neighbors."

They talked late into the evening, and the next day, Kristin began a new outreach effort. She hosted a "meet the dogs" event, invited neighbors to visit the property, and even offered free training sessions for local families.

Meanwhile, Marcus suggested to Justin that they sit down together. The two men who had once butted heads now found common ground—not only in their struggles but in their desire to create something lasting.

As the weeks went on, with Ben's continued encouragement, things began to ease. Kristin's business grew. The neighborhood complaints stopped. And bonds once strained began to strengthen.

They were no longer just living in the same place. They were building a community.

Chapter Eight

Octber arrived with its signature chill, ushering in the scent of wood smoke and the changing colors of the maple trees that lined the neighborhood streets. Kristin's business was flourishing. Her waiting list was growing by the week, and her online reviews, mostly written by delighted clients from surrounding towns, painted her as a gifted dog whisperer and conscientious caretaker.

Inside Kristin's house, tension had crept in around the edges.

Justin, while supportive in theory, had not completely let go of his job loss—or the financial stress that followed. He had not told her that their inheritance was shrinking by the day. He wanted to. He planned to. But every time he saw her smiling face, glowing with pride over the business she had created, he hesitated. He told himself it could wait another day.

Benjamin Pike could sense something was off. He had developed a habit of bringing his dogs to Kristin twice a week so they could socialize with other dogs. One Friday, he arrived to find Justin sitting on the porch, staring into his phone with a distracted look that suggested he wasn't reading anything in particular.

Ben approached cautiously. "Mind some company?"

Justin looked up, startled, but relieved. "Hey, Ben. Yeah, sure. Have a seat."

Ben sat beside him, letting the silence settle first before speaking. "You know, when my wife passed, I thought the hardest part was the silence. But I came to learn the hardest part was pretending everything was fine when it wasn't."

Justin was quiet. His throat tightened.

Ben continued, "You don't have to tell me anything. But if you've got something sitting heavy on you, now's a good time to let a little light in."

It was those words—let a little light in—that did it.

Justin spilled everything. He revisited how devastated he was when he lost his job and all the mistakes he made. The drinking. The mismanagement of money. The shame. And he revealed something he had told no one else. He dropped his head into his hands, expecting judgment. But Ben simply nodded, listening intently.

"I want to tell her about the money," Justin said at last. "I need to. I just . . . don't want to ruin everything."

"You won't ruin anything," Ben replied. "But you will give her the chance to love you as you really are, not just as you pretend to be."

◯◯◯◯◯

Across the street, Pamela was coming to terms with her own internal changes. Her Wednesday afternoons had become quiet rituals—time spent walking through town, journaling, or sometimes just sitting by the pond near the old mill. Ever since her health scare, and the still-unfolding journey with doctors and treatments, she had yearned for deeper clarity, a stronger spiritual footing.

On one of her good days, she met Kristin for tea at the local café. It was supposed to be casual, but within minutes, Kristin confessed she was worried about Justin. "He's been . . . off lately," she admitted, stirring her drink absentmindedly. "Kind of distant."

Pamela hesitated, unsure how much to say. But then she remembered what Ben had told her once—that honesty is a bridge, not a burden.

"He might be afraid," Pamela said gently. "It's not

easy for some men to admit when they're struggling. But I know one thing for sure: he loves you."

Kristin smiled softly. "I hope so."

Later that evening, after putting away dishes and finishing up some client emails, Kristin found Justin sitting on the edge of their bed, looking uncharacteristically serious. She sat beside him, and he took her hand.

"I need to tell you something," he said.

And then he did. For the first time, he opened up about his recent habit of online gambling. "I thought it would be a way to rebuild our savings."

This was a shock that Kristin wasn't prepared for, but she took it in stride.

"Justin, no matter what, we are in this together. I love you, and I always will. Let's get some help."

That night they lay in bed together holding hands, each one shedding silent tears, but with every tear, they felt new strength.

There were many questions to come, and many long walks together under the stars to follow. But there was also understanding. Relief. The kind that comes only from truth being brought into the open.

Ben received two text messages, one from Kristin that read: We're working on spirituality. The one from Justin read: God, Self, and Family. I get it now.

Benjamin wrote a single sentence in his weathered

leather journal: Sometimes the healing begins the moment we stop pretending we don't need it.

$$\textcircled{\text{COOO}}$$

November brought the images of the coming winter. The air took on a crispness that made even simple things—like hot coffee or a morning walk—feel sacred. The rhythm of the town had shifted too. Early signs of the coming holidays appeared in the stores, while several lives in the neighborhood were quietly bracing against personal storms.

For Marcus, the storm was financial. He didn't want to worry Pamela with the latest client losses at the agency. He hid those files from her. She had enough on her plate with her health, and he had convinced himself that if he just worked harder—pushed harder—things would turn around. But they hadn't.

Kristin was facing her own private storm. Her business was thriving by most measures, but she and Justin were still struggling to find their footing. He had his good days, and she felt connected and positive about their future. But then there were the bad days. She was worried that he was still gambling instead of studying. He smiled less. He seemed distant, distracted. She asked him about school, and he brushed her off with vague answers. "Just a lot to learn," he would say. But something in her gut told her it was more than that.

◯◯◯◯

One afternoon, Benjamin stopped by the Marcus' office unannounced. Marcus, surprised by Benjamin's visit, welcomed him and offered coffee. They sat at a small table in the breakroom. The office phones were silent.

"I figured I'd stop in while I was running errands," Ben said. "You've been on my mind."

Marcus offered a smile, but it didn't quite reach his eyes.

Ben leaned in slightly. "How's business, really?"

That was all it took. Marcus exhaled like a balloon deflating. "Honestly, it's been rough. I feel like I'm treading water, and if I stop moving for even a second, I'm going to sink."

Ben listened patiently, nodding. Then he said, "You're not alone. And you don't have to fix everything by yourself. Maybe it's time to bring in someone who thinks differently. Younger. Maybe someone who needs a second chance."

Marcus raised an eyebrow. "You don't mean Justin, do you?"

"I do," Ben said simply. "He's more capable than maybe you give him credit for. And he's floundering. Not because he's weak. Because he's ashamed."

That night, Marcus mentioned it to Pamela. "You

really think that's a good idea?" she asked, stirring soup on the stove.

"I think it might be," Marcus replied. "I know he's got some problems, but he's sharp. Knows numbers. And let's be honest, I could use some fresh energy around here. He told me the other day he doesn't plan to finish law school."

"Wow. That's big. I don't think Kristin knows. She's worried sick about him."

"I think it's worth a discussion. Maybe it won't go anywhere, but I want to try."

Meanwhile, across the street, Kristin had made her own decision. She couldn't keep pretending everything was fine. That evening after dinner, she asked Justin to sit down.

"I need you to be honest with me," she said gently. "Whatever it is you're carrying, I want to help you carry it."

There was a long silence. Then, as if the dam had finally cracked, Justin dropped the latest bombshell. He admitted he was flunking out of law school and had started gambling again.

"I've messed up so bad, Kris. You probably want a divorce."

She knelt before him and took his hands in hers.

"Never. We are in this together, and I believe in my heart things are about to change. I need you to believe in yourself, because I believe in you."

⊂⊃⊂⊃⊂⊃

Some weeks later, all four of them sat around Benjamin Pike's kitchen table. He'd invited them for a casual dinner, but they knew it was more than that. It always was with Ben.

"You know," he said, pouring wine into their glasses, "we think we need more time. More money. More answers. But what we really need—what we always need—is more truth. More honesty. And more courage to build a life that's aligned with our values."

He looked around the table.

"You've each been given an invitation," he said. "To reset. To choose differently. Not out of guilt or fear, but out of hope. Abundance doesn't show up in your bank account. It shows up in the choices you make every day to become more fully yourself."

Kristin reached for Justin's hand.

Pamela touched Marcus's arm.

And Ben—the quiet mentor, humble guide, wise friend—smiled. The storms hadn't passed. But now, at least, no one was standing in them alone.

For the next four hours, they shared their hopes, their dreams, their fears, and from that came solutions.

Marcus raised his glass to toast, "To great friends. To new partnerships. To successful ventures. And to good health."

"Here. Here." In unison, everyone took a drink.

Pamela winked at Marcus. "I guess I should tell them." He nodded. "I just got the call from my doctor today. He says I'm going to be fine. I still have to finish another round of chemotherapy, but I don't need surgery."

"That's wonderful!" Kristin ran to Pamela's side and gave her a big hug and kiss.

Justin stood, "I have never felt so positive about my life, my marriage, and my future. Ben, thank you for helping me see that when I shifted my paradigm, I was able to focus on the right things. I know I'm on the path to living an abundant life."

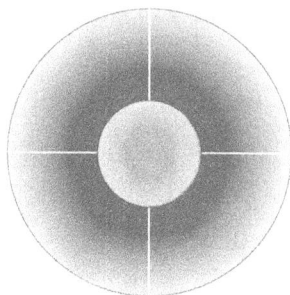

Chapter Nine

S
pring gave way to summer, and the energy surrounding Kristin's new business surged. Flyers went out to local dog owners, and her social media presence—thanks to her friend Amy's tech savvy—was drawing impressive engagement. Her closest neighbors all had a dog now and, of course, Kristin's service catered to all of them while they went to work every day. On weekends, she invited them to stop by and participate in the training sessions. Kristin felt momentum building, and she remained cautiously optimistic.

One afternoon, after a long session of obedience drills and fetch games, Kristin received a visit she didn't expect: Pamela.

She was holding a Tupperware container of lemon squares.

"For the trainer and her troops," she said with a wink.

Kristin smiled, brushing the dog fur off her jeans. "You're a lifesaver."

They sat on the back deck overlooking the training yard, Thor and Zeus dozing nearby in the sun.

Pamela looked out over the space thoughtfully.

"You've really made something here," she said. "It's not just about the dogs. It's got purpose."

Kristin glanced down. "That's what I'm hoping. But it's not always easy. I sense there are still people who don't like the fact that I'm running this business here."

Pamela nodded. "That's actually why I came. I think I can help."

She told Kristin about a meeting Marcus had recently attended at the community association, where some concerns were voiced yet again—not angrily, but with frustration. The uptick in traffic, the barking—it wasn't yet a crisis, but it was growing.

Kristin's heart sank, but Pamela reached for her hand. "Listen. This is your moment to invite them in. Host an open house for the people you don't know. Let them see what you're building—not just as a business, but as something good for the neighborhood. And I think you should reach out to folks beyond our street."

Kristin took a breath. "You really think that'll make a difference?"

"I think you've already made a difference. You just need them to see it."

⬭⬭⬭⬭

Two days later, Kristin called Ben. "Can we talk?" she asked. "I could use your insight."

Of course, he said. They met in his orchard once again.

She walked him through everything—business progress, neighbor tension, Pamela's suggestion.

Ben, ever calm, nodded as he listened.

"It feels like for every step I make forward, something pushes me back."

"Let me ask you something," he said when she finished. "Do you believe this business of yours could contribute to the well-being of the people around you, not just their pets?"

Kristin hesitated. "I don't know. I never really asked myself that. But now that I think about it, yes. I really do."

"Then you don't need to convince them. You need to show them."

And that was the nudge she needed.

They planned the event for the following Saturday. Justin helped hang banners and set up folding chairs, while Amy created colorful handouts and a digital RSVP form. Kristin personally invited every neighbor on their street and the surrounding streets, even the ones on the opposite side of the golf course.

On the day of the event, the backyard buzzed with laughter, tail-wagging chaos, and community chatter. Parents with children petted puppies, elderly couples smiled and shared stories about dogs they once owned, and neighbors who hadn't spoken in months found themselves laughing over spilled dog treats.

And Pamela and her lead trainer put on a demonstration with the dogs who just graduated from her Puppy Plus training program.

Marcus and Pamela arrived hand-in-hand. They walked over to Ben, who was seated in the shade sipping iced tea.

"You were right," Marcus said. "She just needed to show them."

Ben raised his glass slightly. "Abundance has a funny way of multiplying when it's shared."

By sunset, as the last guests drifted home and the dogs finally curled up in exhaustion, Kristin sat on the deck with Justin, Ben, and the Stephens. They had built a foundation of trust.

And it would carry them forward, one circle at a time.

Autumn settled over New Canaan with a kind of

gentle insistence—the air crisper, the evenings cooler, the golden trees dropping their leaves like reminders to let go.

And in that spirit, Marcus did just that. After Justin left law school, Marcus brought up the idea of giving insurance a try. It turned out to be a great decision for both of them.

He had always clung tightly to control his business, his finances, his schedule. But lately, with Justin's help, he was learning to loosen his grip. Not to give up, but to let in help.

"We are holding our own, but we need to do more," Justin said. "I have some ideas I'd like to run by you."

"Bring it on. I'm all ears," Marcus said.

Justin used the whiteboard in the back conference room to sketch out a digital marketing strategy, and by the end of the day, the two men had a plan. Justin, who was brought in as a minority partner, would help modernize the agency's operations and lead generation. And Marcus would stay focused on sales.

When Marcus told Pamela that night, she said. "I told you. You just needed someone who sees the big picture, the future."

"I thought that was supposed to be me," he replied, half-joking.

"You've been carrying too much," she said. "Now maybe you can breathe again."

Since the community gathering, Kristin's business was not only thriving—it was becoming a small sensation. A write-up in a local lifestyle blog about her "boutique canine wellness center" led to inquiries from neighboring towns. She was fielding calls from pet owners willing to drive an hour or more for her services.

But she didn't want expansion to cost her the community she had built—so she went to the one person she knew would give honest, grounded advice.

Benjamin Pike.

They met on her back porch, where she served a fresh pot of cinnamon tea and laid out a plate of ginger cookies. Kristin sat across from him, grateful for the moment of calm.

"I'm worried," she admitted. "Now things are happening fast. Too fast. I don't want to lose what matters in the name of growth."

Ben nodded thoughtfully, stirring his tea. "There's a question I like to ask myself," he said. "Will this decision bring me closer to the life I want, or further away?"

Kristin mulled that over.

"I think I want to expand. I've got the room, but I don't want to become . . . impersonal."

"Then don't," Ben said simply. "Grow in a way that matches your values. Hire the right people. Build systems that protect the culture you've created. And always leave room for people—clients, team, neighbors. That's the real business you're in."

She smiled. "You always make it sound so obvious."

"It is. But obvious doesn't mean easy."

"Somehow I knew you'd say that." Kristin stood on tiptoes and gave Ben a peck on the cheek as he moved to leave. "I can always count on you."

That weekend, the Marchans hosted a backyard dinner for their closest neighbors—Marcus and Pamela, of course, but also Stan and Cindy, her new employees, and even a few clients who had become friends. It was casual and warm, with string lights swaying gently above the patio and the two German Shepherds lounging calmly near the fire pit.

At one point, Pamela leaned over to Kristin and whispered, "Remember when this all started? When we didn't know what to make of each other?"

Kristin laughed. "I remember you looked at me like I had dropped in from another planet."

"I probably did," Pamela said. "But now . . . I can't imagine this neighborhood without you."

Justin brought out a tray of ingredients to make s'mores over the fire, and Marcus was telling a story that had everyone laughing hard enough to forget the chill in the air.

Ben wasn't there that night. He was visiting his daughter in Boston. But his presence was unmistakable— woven into the connections, the conversations, the quiet wisdom they all now carried with them.

By the time the fire burned low, and the last plates were cleared, it was obvious to everyone: something had changed. Not in a dramatic way, but in the small, powerful kind of way that means the world will never quite go back to how it was.

They had become a circle.

And within that circle, they were learning— together—how to live not just successfully, but abundantly.

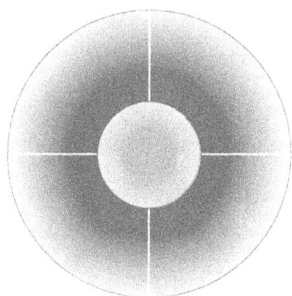

Chapter Ten

The first snow fell in early December, a quiet, silencing blanket that softened the landscape and slowed the pace of the town. Sparkling lights began appearing in windows, wreaths on doors, and the faint scent of pine and cinnamon seemed to drift on the wind. New Canaan, like many places in New England, transforms in winter—not just physically, but spiritually. There was a sense of stillness, of reflection, and this year, that mood seemed to touch everyone in their little circle more deeply than usual.

For Marcus, the season brought a surprising surge of clients—families looking to update policies before the new year, retirees seeking advice, young couples needing guidance on their next . With Justin by his side, the agency felt reborn. There was laughter in the office now, fresh ideas flying across desks, and a deeper sense of purpose that extended beyond closing a deal.

"What we're really offering," Justin said during one team meeting, "is peace of mind and a stable future for our clients. Let's treat it like that."

Meanwhile, Pamela was returning to her old self. She felt stronger even though she wasn't completely out of the woods. The grandkids came by twice a week to visit after school, and she filled their time with reading, games, and crafts. Kristin came over whenever she could, sometimes just to sit with her and chat about nothing in particular. Sometimes she would even bring Zeus and Thor, who were now best friends with Suzy and Sammy.

One snowy afternoon, Ben stopped by with a paper bag of groceries and a bundle of firewood under one arm. He never asked Pam if she needed anything. He simply showed up.

"Pamela," he said, placing the firewood by the hearth, "you're too dignified to admit it, but I know you don't always take care of yourself when you don't have someone to cook for. So, I brought you my chicken barley soup. It's not fancy, but Margaret used to say it was my best version of manna from heaven."

Pamela took the container. "Thank you, Ben. This means more than I can say."

He stayed for an hour, long enough to share a story about the time he and Marcus once got lost during a chamber of commerce retreat in the Berkshires, and the entire group howled with laughter. "When we emerged from the woods two hours later, we were greeted with open arms. . It was a gift, that visit. A reminder that life could be heavy, but it could still hold joy."

⟨⟨⟨⟨⟩

Across the street, Kristin was making another big decision: to formally rebrand her business. She wanted a name that reflected not just dog care, but the mission behind it. After weeks of brainstorming, she settled on Pawthway—a nod to both the dogs and the journey they helped guide their owners through. Underneath the logo, she added a simple tagline: "For lives well-lived—yours and theirs."

She planned to launch the new branding with a holiday fundraiser for the local animal shelter, bringing together clients, neighbors, and fellow small business owners for a day of giving back. Ben told her that a life well lived included generosity, not just gratitude. Justin would run the donation table. Stan would serve the food (for people and dogs alike). And since it was still warm, Cindy would run agility demos with some of the more trainable pups. And Kristin envisioned herself standing under a banner with her new logo. Just the feeling gave her something she hadn't felt in a long time: certainty.

This was what she was meant to do.

Ben attended the event, of course. He spent most of the afternoon sipping hot tea and chatting with anyone who sat beside him on the folding bench he'd staked out on the back deck. As usual, his words weren't many—but they were always enough. He told Kristin her new name was brilliant. Told Justin he was proud of how far he'd come. Told Amy she should consider applying to a PhD program in marketing. "Pawthway is brilliant. You've got more creative talent in you than you realize," he said. Amy blushed at the compliment.

Later that evening, Justin looked across the dinner table and said quietly, "You know... I think we're becoming the people we were supposed to be."

Kristin smiled at him, her eyes glinting in the candlelight. "I think we always were. We just had to stop pretending to be someone else."

And in that quiet moment, as the snow began to fall again outside, they both knew: abundance wasn't about perfection. It was about alignment. It was about choosing, again and again, to build something lasting—together.

⦿⦿⦿⦿

At the Stephens household, things were also beginning to transform. Pamela started journaling again, but now with a new purpose. Maybe her experience with cancer could help others someday. With Kristin's encouragement and Ben's ongoing insight, she began reflecting on what gave her joy beyond work and daily responsibilities.

When Marcus came home one evening to find her painting in the sunroom, he smiled. "Didn't know we had a new artist in the house."

She laughed. "Just following Ben's advice. Tending to my personal circle."

That night over dinner they talked like they hadn't in years. Dreams. The future. And the possibility of transferring the business to Justin at some point. Marcus shared his confidence in Justin and how impressed he was by the younger man's ideas. They had a clearer vision for what abundance could look like.

CCCCO

Ben met with the two men the following week and offered guidance on forming a formal full partnership that honored both experience and innovation. It also provided for a buyout so Justin could take over the business when Marcus retired. "Legacy is about transfer," he said. "Knowledge, values, purpose—not just assets."

Justin was already investing in the business with sweat equity and now through a financial formula that would lead to taking over the business when Marcus was ready to retire. With his new role as partner, he felt a renewed sense of purpose.

Two more seasons passed. Ben's influence was everywhere—not loud, not flashy, but present. He believed leadership is influence. A leader teaches others how to think so they can do what they need to do to get what they want. He planted seeds of growth in every conversation. Helping each person see that the abundant life wasn't about perfection, but about wholeness.

And that wholeness was beginning to blossom.

One Saturday morning, Marcus stopped by the orchard alone. Ben greeted him near the shed, where he was sorting baskets of newly harvested peaches.

"You're here early," Ben said with a knowing glance.

Marcus looked weathered, but hopeful. "Couldn't sleep. Too much on my mind."

They walked together down a shaded path, eventually settling on a bench that overlooked the orchard.

"I just want to get things right," Marcus admitted. "With Pam, with the business, with everything."

"Tell me something," Ben said. "What do you think Pam needs most right now?"

Marcus didn't hesitate. "Support. Reassurance. Faith."

Ben nodded. "Then that's where your abundance starts."

"Is this leadership or abundance?" Marcus asked.

"Sometimes leadership is just support. It's about having intentional conversations . . . listening."

Marcus nodded. "She has been my rock throughout our entire marriage. I have always been so focused on the business that I look back now and realize I took her for granted. I don't know what I'd do if I lost her."

Ben reassured Marcus. "There is no chance of that. Pam loves you. But right now, her foundation is still a bit shaky. I would talk to her and just listen. I'm willing to bet there isn't anything she needs you to do as much as that . . . just listen."

Marcus picked up a peach and bit into it. He wiped the juice from his chin with the back of his hand. He smacked his lips. "Now, that is enough to give a man renewed energy. I can use it. The business is looking stronger every day, and now I have to balance my time between that and Pamela."

"Do you?" Ben asked. "Marcus, you are a man who prides himself on doing everything. Do you trust Justin to take on even more responsibility?

"Absolutely. He has been amazing. He's a fast learner and so motivated to keep his life on the right path. He has great ideas."

"Then, my friend, I suggest you get out of the way and give him room to run. My prediction is it will not only help the business, but it will give you that extra time to spend with the most important person in your life. Right now, the circles you need to give attention to are personal and family."

Kristin gave herself a quiet moment of reflection that same day. She walked her property alone after closing shop for the afternoon. Thor and Zeus padded beside her, tails wagging. As she looked around at what she had built, she felt both pride and a pang of worry. Justin had been quiet lately. She knew from Pamela that things were going well at the insurance agency, but something still weighed heavily on him.

After dinner that evening, she brought it up.

"I want to know what's really going on," she said. "Not with us, but with you."

Justin hesitated, then finally opened up. "I can't seem to let go of all my mistakes. I'm still ashamed. About the money I lost. About how I handled things."

Kristin reached for his hand. "Shame fixes nothing. But honesty can. I married you, not your balance sheet. We are rebuilding this together. Are you happy about your decision to go into business with Marcus?"

"Yes, of course. He is a great mentor, and I'm finding I have a knack for insurance."

"But there's something else. What is it, Justin?"

He stared at her, his eyes swimming with tears. "I

was looking at my notes from one of our meetings with Ben. Here's the thing. I feel good about the progress I've made personally. I know we are doing great. I know I can earn the money back, and I even feel pretty good about the progress we're making with our community. I even got invited to play golf next week with three other guys who live in our neighborhood."

"I'm hearing you. But the piece that is missing is spiritual." Pam lifted his chin to place a delicate kiss on his lips.

"How did you know? Is that crazy?"

"Not at all. In fact, I've been having the same feelings. When I was driving to town the other day, for the first time I noticed every church I passed. St. Mark's Episcopal, The Congregational Church, and the Methodist Church. It was like they were daring me to stop. I felt this strange, almost magnetic pull." Kristin shook her head.

"I had something weird happen too. I was driving down Park St., and a deer ran across the road right in front of the Congregational Church. I had to slam on the brakes to avoid hitting it. When I caught my breath, I looked up, and the pastor was standing in the doorway and gave me a wave and a thumbs up. My guilt meter shot off the charts because I knew he knew we had stopped coming to church. I waved back but kept on going. Maybe it's a sign."

Kristin agreed. "If it is, it's a good one! It's been way too long. Even with all she's been going through, Pam and Marcus never miss a Sunday. We have focused on the other areas of life. While they are becoming more successful, it doesn't seem to be fulfilling."

"Then I say we go this Sunday. We talked about how important church and finding our spirituality were when we first got married, but we never followed through. I keep reflecting on the fact that Ben told us that a life well lived is having abundance in all 5 circles. It requires intentional growth."

Kristin nodded and picked up her phone. "Pam, it's Kris. Would you be open to Justin and I going to church with you and Marcus on Sunday?"

A minute later, she clicked off and turned to Justin. "It's all set. And guess what? Ben is preaching this Sunday! This is more than a sign. This is the next important step on our spiritual journey."

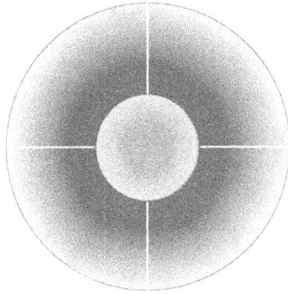

Chapter Eleven

F all gave way to winter, and the holidays arrived
with a hush and a glow. Snow clung to rooftops and
sparkled under streetlamps. Windows glimmered
with soft light. And within the hearts of the people who
had drawn closer over the past year, there was a new
rhythm—a steadier one.

On Christmas Eve, Benjamin Pike opened his home
again—not for a party, but for what he called a "quiet
celebration." Just close friends, simple food, and a
fire that crackled in the stone hearth like an old friend
humming a lullaby.

Marcus wrapped a handmade shawl around Pam's
shoulders that he grabbed before they left the house. It
was navy blue with tiny gold threads, woven by a local
artisan he found after a long search. "For strength," he

told her. "And warmth." Pamela had just completed her final round of treatment and, though thinner and a little frail, she moved with a calmness that came only from the strength that comes from surviving something harrowing.

The Marchans arrived at Ben's, Kristin carrying a basket of freshly baked muffins, Justin lugging a bottle of Cabernet and two gift bags that clearly weren't wrapped by him.

"Another Christmas together," Justin remarked as they stepped inside. "It feels . . . right."

"Feels like we are home; that we belong," Kristin added, slipping out of her coat.

Cindy and Stan rolled in right after Justin and Kristin. They were part of the community that gravitated to Ben. Stan brought a hand-carved wooden ornament for Ben's tree. "Just a little thank you," he said. "For all your stories and your steady way."

Ben didn't say much in response. He just smiled, gave Stan a long hug, and hung the ornament on a bough where everyone could see it.

As the evening settled into that soft cadence only winter nights seem to know, conversation turned once again—not surprisingly—to purpose. To priorities. To what each of them wanted from the year ahead.

Ben, in his usual gentle way, asked a question that no one answered right away.

"What will be your word for the coming year?"
They looked at him.

"Not a resolution," he said. "A word. One that sets your compass. That grounds you when the world tries to pull you off course."

Pamela leaned into Marcus. "I think mine is 'grace.'"

Kristin considered. "Maybe 'build.' Not just the business, but a life that matters."

Justin nodded slowly. "Mine might be 'integrity.' I want to choose to live closer to my values."

Stan, surprisingly, said, "Mine's 'listen.' I spend so much time talking. I think now I want to hear more."

Cindy said, "My word is 'joy.' Just being here with all of you fills my heart with joy."

Ben turned to Marcus.

"Legacy," Marcus said. "That's mine. It's time." He put his arm around Pam. "Who knows? I might even be in the market for a boat." He winked at Justin.

They were quiet for a while, each staring into the crackling fire, lost in their own thoughts.

Ben took a sip of cider and finally offered his own. "Stewardship." After a beat, he added. "I want to add leadership and relationships. I think the world would be a different place if more people asked themselves each morning, What am I stewarding today? A relationship? A decision? A moment that matters?"

Outside, the wind brushed against the windowpanes.

Inside, the warmth of the room wasn't just from the fire—it was from the knowing. The sense that in this small town, in this small circle, something significant was growing.

Not fame.

Not fortune.

But meaning.

Connection.

Abundance.

As the night drew to a close and everyone gathered their coats before saying soft goodbyes, Kristin turned to Ben and said, "You always know just what to say."

Ben smiled kindly. "Not always. But I've learned when to ask the right question."

⦿⦿⦿⦿

Over the coming months, there were many more coffee dates, visits to Ben's orchard, laughter from neighborhood gatherings, and long conversations.

September ushered in a new kind of rhythm. The days shortened, the leaves turned brittle and golden, and across New Canaan, people began preparing for the inevitable hibernation that autumn in New England gently demanded. But for the Marchans and the Stephens, change no longer felt like something to brace against. It felt, instead like something to welcome.

Marcus had taken a step he once would have avoided:

he was letting go. Pamela had finished her treatments with quiet strength and resilience, and she was strong. The partnership with Justin brought fresh ideas into the agency—ideas that were bearing fruit. Pam returned to work two days a week and helped launch a new social media campaign, modernized their client onboarding. Those efforts were reaching a younger demographic that Marcus had never quite known how to access before.

One crisp afternoon, Ben stopped by the agency with a basket of apples from his orchard. He set it down on the conference table, smiling.

"Just a little reminder that growth takes time," he said.

Justin looked up from his laptop. "We're getting there. Slowly but surely."

Marcus nodded. "I challenge you on slow, partner. We're making amazing progress, more than I could have ever hoped for, or could have done on my own."

Meanwhile, Kristin was preparing for something entirely new: her first public seminar. She would hold the seminar at the community center; it was a free event titled "Purpose Through Passion: Building a Meaningful Life by Doing What You Love." The idea started as a suggestion from Pamela, and then Ben encouraged it, too. "You have a voice," he told Kristin. "You've built something with heart. People need to hear how you did it."

On the night of the seminar, Kristin stood before the small but eager audience—neighbors, pet lovers, young entrepreneurs—she was nervous, but her voice steadied as soon as she began. She spoke of beginnings, mistakes, reinvention, and the importance of vision—of taking risks—of learning from the dogs she trained.

Justin stood at the back of the room next to the door, where he could direct people as they arrived. He beamed with pride as Kristin shared her story . . . their story.

When it was over, the applause overwhelmed her. It gave her a renewed sense of satisfaction. Kristin realized then that something in her had blossomed. She wasn't just building a business anymore. She was building her own legacy, and she was making a difference.

Benjamin sat quietly in the back row until everyone else was gone. Afterward, he approached her with a simple compliment. "You gave people something to believe in tonight. Don't ever stop."

⚬⚬⚬⚬

Marcus and Pamela couldn't attend that night because they were on the last day of their Caribbean cruise.

To make up for it, when they returned, they invited Ben and the Marchans over for dinner. Pamela was radiant and feeling one hundred percent like her old self. She wanted to celebrate—with something small, something meaningful. The conversation at the table ranged from the recap of Kristin's event, to football, to faith, from the best apple pie crust recipe, to long-term plans.

After dinner, Marcus refreshed the blazing fire in the fireplace, and the friends gathered around sipping mulled cider and munching on Pamela's apple cider doughnuts.

Eventually, the conversation turned once more to dreams. Not the lofty, abstract kind. But the kind you whisper late at night, when you feel safe.

"I used to think dreams had an expiration date," Marcus admitted. "But now I'm starting to believe they just take on new forms."

Pamela nodded. "Sometimes they get interrupted, but that doesn't mean they die. They adapt."

Justin added, "Or sometimes, they're waiting for the right people to help make them real."

Ben finally spoke. "You know, we all spend a lot of time chasing what we think life should be. But maybe the better question is: what does it mean to live well? Not perfectly. Just well. With intention. With love. With community."

Kristin smiled. "And maybe with a few dogs at your side."

They laughed, but something in the air had settled over the group—a quiet acknowledgment of what they were all building together. It wasn't flashy. It wasn't simple. But it was real. Lost in their own thoughts, they each realized that relationships were important along with their commitment to intentional growth.

As the night wound down, Pamela walked Ben to the door. "You know, you've been more than just a friend to us. You've been a compass."

Ben looked at her, eyes kind. "We all get lost sometimes. The trick is walking with people who help you find your way back."

She hugged him tightly.

In the weeks that followed, more good news came. Kristin won the Best New Business award from the town of New Canaan; Justin sold his biggest insurance policy yet for one of his golf buddies' businesses. Marcus was taking time off every week to volunteer for Meals on Wheels. And Pamela's latest scan showed she was clear of cancer.

The 5 circles that Ben always spoke about—Spiritual, Personal, Family, Community, and Financial—had become more than a framework.

They had become a focus.

And that life, messy and beautiful and full of unexpected turns, was, at last, abundant.

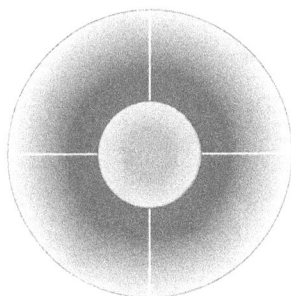

Chapter Twelve

One afternoon, the men were gathered at Ben's house. They had started meeting regularly a few months before. Ben had the fire burning in the fireplace when they arrived, and he served mismatched bowls of lentil stew with crusty bread. As they sat down, Ben spoke. "I've been thinking about something. About thresholds."

"Thresholds?" Marcus asked.

Ben nodded. "It's that moment when something ends and something else begins. A line. A doorway. And what I've learned is that we rarely recognize we're standing on one until we're already through it."

Marcus and Justin sipped their soup but didn't speak. They waited for Ben to continue.

"I think all three of us have crossed a few thresholds together—careers, health, dreams shifting, identities changing. That's no small thing. But it's also an invitation."

"An invitation to what?" Justin asked.

"To reimagine what comes next," Ben said. "And not just based on what's urgent—but based on what's meaningful. What matters. What you truly want."

Marcus set down his spoon. "I used to think meaning came from big moments—milestones, achievements, celebrations. Now, I think it comes from smaller things. Like waking up to the smell of coffee brewing. Or the sound of the garage door opening when Pam returns from the store. I went years without noticing those things."

Ben nodded. "You've crossed a very important threshold, my friend."

"I know what you mean, Marcus. Since Kristin and I started going back to church, I'm tuned into things that I never experienced before; like the sound of her voice when she's singing the hymns, or the touch of her hand when we recite the Lord's Prayer. Is this what you call a spiritual awakening, Ben?"

"It is that and more. What you are describing are thresholds to a deeper connection that will bring abundance in those areas of life that matter most to you. Whether it's spiritual, personal, family, financial, or community, you have embarked on your own personal journey. Abundance requires intentional growth, and your intentions have brought you to where you are."

The snow outside had stopped, and the sun streamed in the windows.

"Here's what I hope for each of you," Ben said. "That you keep walking forward, even when the road is unclear. That you build lives not just around what you do, but who you are—and who you love. That you keep asking: How do I live well? And that you remember the answer isn't something you find once. It's something you live into, over time."

The men were quiet for a while after that. Not because there was nothing left to say, but because what had just been said needed space to settle.

When it was time to leave, Justin reached out his hand and pulled Ben into a bear hug. "Thank you," he whispered.

"For what?"

"For seeing me. For seeing us. For helping us see ourselves."

Marcus added, "I couldn't have said it better."

Ben chuckled. "That's what friends are for."

$$\text{(O)(O)(O)}$$

Mornings were cooler, leaves blazed in oranges and crimsons, and routines grew steadier. But for the

Marchans, the Stephens, and the friends orbiting their circle, it wasn't just the weather that was changing.

Something deeper was taking root.

Kristin was walking through her kennel one golden October morning, clipboard in hand, when she spotted Ben leaning against the fence. He had a way of showing up just when people didn't know they needed him.

"This is a surprise. Here for an inspection?" she called out, grinning.

Ben returned the smile. "Just passing by. Figured I'd check in on the empire."

Kristin walked over. "We've added three new clients this week," she said. "And next month, I'm starting a weekend training course for teens who want to learn how to work with dogs. They get community service hours, school credit—plus, I know the dogs will love it."

Ben nodded with quiet approval. "You've turned purpose into practice. That's harder than it sounds."

Kristin looked down suddenly modest. "Some days I'm still making it up as I go."

Ben leaned on the fence post. "Aren't we all?"

⊙⊙⊙⊙

Across town, Justin was deep in spreadsheets and sales reports, his sleeves rolled up in the office he shared with Marcus. They had carved out a rhythm—a surprising balance of old-school wisdom and new-school momentum. For Marcus, what had once felt like a business nearing the end of its arc now felt more like a beginning.

At lunch that day, over takeout sandwiches at his desk, Marcus leaned back and looked over at Justin.

"You know, I didn't think I'd be excited about work again at my age," he said.

Justin smiled. "And I didn't think I'd ever enjoy actuarial tables."

They both laughed.

Marcus grew more thoughtful. "You've got vision, Justin. But more than that, you've got humility now. That's not something a business course can teach you."

"I had to lose a few things to gain it," Justin agreed.

⬤⬤⬤⬤

Later that afternoon, Pamela stopped by Kristin's with a basket of muffins and a sparkle in her eyes. She wanted to share her idea of talking with the community center about launching a support group for women navigating illness and identity at the same time.

"I've realized something," Pamela told Kristin as they sipped tea in the backyard. "You don't wait until everything's perfect to start living well. You live through the mess. The abundance isn't after the storm. It's in how you walk through it."

Kristin nodded. "I think that's exactly what Ben's been trying to teach all of us."

⦿⦿⦿⦿

That Sunday, Marcus and Pamela invited Ben, Kristin and Justin over for an informal dinner—just soup and bread and stories. The fire crackled in the stone hearth as the night chill blanketed the town and stars blinked to life outside the window.

After dinner, they moved to the family room to sit close to the fire. Pam served hot cocoa and divine butter cookies from the local bakery.

Marcus asked, "What shall we mull over tonight?"

"I have a question. What's the next step?" Kristin asked. "Once you find balance, what do you do with it?"

Ben looked around at their faces, lit by firelight. "You share it," he said simply. "You mentor. You lift. You build bridges. Abundance isn't something you hoard. It's something you pass along."

He paused, letting his words settle.

"We've talked a lot about the 5 circles—Spiritual, Personal, Family, Community, Financial—but what we don't say often enough is that they're not just about us. They're how we give to others. Through faith, encouragement, support, opportunity, and stewardship." Ben laced his fingers over his chest, allowing the impact of his words to sink in.

Pamela reached over and squeezed his hand. "So, what you're saying is . . . it's not just a life well-lived."

"It is about a life well-lived, but there's more. It's a legacy," Ben said. "And it starts now."

Silence followed—the warm kind that confirms something real has just been said.

Outside, leaves rustled. Inside, logs shifted in the fire. And in that moment, all 5 of them knew something that went beyond plans or progress. They were no longer just recovering from what had happened. They were stepping forward into the bigger vision of what they were creating.

As individuals, as couples, and as friends—together.

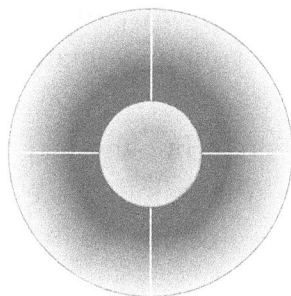

Chapter Thirteen

Leaves spiraled to the ground in burnt-orange choreography, and the chill in the air turned morning coffee into a small ritual. With the season of abundance behind them, the families that once danced on the edges of misunderstanding had grown into something new: a true community.

Kristin's business was not just successful, but respected. Several neighbors who had once raised concerns were now loyal clients, impressed by the professionalism and care she brought to each animal and each interaction. One of them, Shirley Parker—a self-appointed guardian of neighborhood propriety—even publicly complimented Kristin during a recent town meeting. She was on the docket to renew her business permit. "I was skeptical at first," Shirley confessed, "but

I've never seen a cleaner, better-run facility. And frankly, it's good to see a young woman doing something meaningful."

Kristin was floored. But she had learned to accept compliments with the same grace she used when navigating criticism: calmly, without letting either dictate her worth.

Meanwhile, at the agency, Marcus and Justin had struck a rhythm that was working. Where Marcus brought gravitas and hard-earned wisdom, Justin added energy, optimism, and a tech-savvy edge. They had formally welcomed Charles Wycoff, a bright young man Marcus had first brought on as a summer intern but was unable to retain when he graduated because of declining business. Charles showed great promise with his natural sales ability and empathy towards his clients. Marcus acted as his mentor and took him on sales calls to help him develop his own book of business, while Justin included him in strategy meetings.

Pamela herself had taken a different leap. She began mentoring younger women at Norwalk Hospital—those newly diagnosed with life-threatening illnesses, uncertain and scared. Her presence was a balm: warm, steady, rooted in an empathy that can't be faked.

⬤⬤⬤⬤⬤

One afternoon in late October, Ben sent a text to all four of them. Don't make any plans Saturday. We're going on a Vision Walk.

Kristin was the first to respond to the group text. What's that?

Meet me at the trailhead at 9am, he'd texted back, with no other explanation.

Curious but trusting, they arrived: Kristin in leggings and a hoodie, Justin carrying a thermos of coffee, Marcus in a well-worn flannel, and Pamela wrapped in a cozy shawl, cheeks rosy with anticipation.

"We're going for a walk?" Justin asked, eyebrows raised.

"A walk," Ben confirmed, eyes twinkling. "But also, a conversation."

The trail was quiet, carpeted in dry leaves. As they hiked the path, Ben posed a question to each of them.

"Kristin," he said, "what legacy are you building that will outlast your business?"

She paused, taken aback. "I've never thought about that. I think . . . no, I know . . . I want people to remember me as someone who created connection. Not just between people and dogs, but between people and their purpose."

Ben nodded and turned to Pamela. "And you? What does resilience look like in your next ?"

Pamela smiled gently. "Resilience used to mean

getting through the hard days. Now it means being fully present on the good ones."

Marcus and Justin were quiet as they walked, taking in the deepening colors of the trees. Then Ben asked Marcus, "How does leadership change when it's no longer about control?"

Marcus laughed. "It becomes about trust. About knowing when to let go so others can rise." He shot a knowing glance at Justin.

Finally, Ben turned to Justin. "What does redemption look like when you're experiencing transformation spiritually?"

Justin took a moment before answering. "It looks like peace. And a chance to help someone else not fall into the same trap."

The trail curved around a ridge where the view opened up—a wide expanse of rolling hills painted in gold and rust. They stopped and stood there in silence for a long moment.

"This," Ben said, gesturing to the view, "is what happens when change is embraced instead of feared. When each part of your life speaks to the others."

He turned to face them. "You each have lived through upheaval. But you didn't break. You built. Now the question is, what are you building next?"

Nobody answered right away. But they didn't need to. The seeds had been planted, and each of them knew it. Their stories weren't finished. Their circles hadn't closed. They were only widening.

As the sun dipped lower in the October sky, they turned and began the walk back. Together. Not as survivors, or even just neighbors. But as visionaries, quietly committed to living lives of depth, purpose, and abundance—not someday, but now.

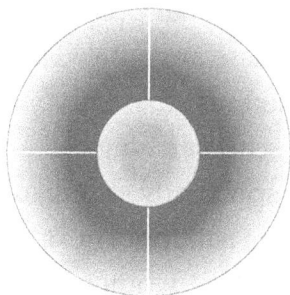

Chapter Fourteen

Thanksgiving was only a week away, but the weather remained unusually warm, so Ben decided to invite some of his friends over to celebrate—not for a party, not for a seminar, not even for a dog training demo. They came just to be together. To mark the end of one season and to welcome in the beginning of another.

Kristin took Ben's idea one step further. She wanted this to be a community appreciation event, open to neighbors, clients, families, and friends. She assigned duties to everyone to bring cider and apple fritters, potluck dishes, hay bales and picnic blankets, and more.

Marcus and Justin stood near one of the orchard trees, talking shop—only this time, their conversation had less to do with sales targets and more to do with shared values and personal purpose. They weren't just co-owners of a business anymore. They were allies.

Pamela watched as the kids played freeze tag, laughing, her blue scarf catching the wind like a sail. She felt physically and spiritually strong, better than she had in a long time. Kristin sat down next to her, carrying two mugs of cocoa. The two women roared with laughter when the dogs joined in. Challenge, not convenience, forged the bond between these two women.

When things died down, Benjamin stepped onto a small wooden platform Kristin and Justin had set up beneath the oldest apple tree on the property. It was her idea, and she wanted it to be special. "Say a few words," she urged, "for everyone."

He looked out at the faces—young and old, familiar and new—and felt a peace settle over him.

"Thank you for coming," he began. "This orchard has seen many seasons. Some harsh. Some abundant. What I've learned is that we don't get to choose the weather. But we do get to choose how we grow through it."

He paused, looking at the people who had come into his life unexpectedly—neighbors, friends, seekers, survivors.

"I once believed that wisdom came from solitude," he continued. "And maybe, for a while, it does. But the kind that changes lives—the kind that heals, that builds, that expands us—it only comes through connection. For years, you've heard me talk about the 5 circles we all share—spiritual, personal, family, community, and financial. We know there is not one above the other. They work together, supporting one another."

He took a slow breath.

"Living an abundant life doesn't mean we never face setbacks. It means we don't face them alone."

There was silence, not the awkward kind, but the kind that came from people absorbing something they felt deep in their bones. Then, one by one, the crowd began to applaud.

Kristin stepped on the platform beside Ben. She reached up and gave him a kiss on the cheek. "Ben, we're all here for another reason today. It is to thank you for all you have done for us."

"Here! Here!" Other voices joined Marcus, Justin and Pamela.

She continued, "You have given us hope, and wisdom, and helped us realize what our lives can and should be. I speak for everyone in saying that you have opened our eyes to all that is possible and guided us on our journey to a well-lived, abundant life."

For once, Ben was at a loss for words. He let the tears stream down his cheeks and mouthed the words "Thank you."

After everyone left, Benjamin Pike stood alone next to that old apple tree, surveying his orchard—he saw the faces of his community—and what he had always hoped to see—for himself and everyone around him.

A life well lived.

A harvest shared.

A future unfolding.

And in that moment, under that twilight sky, everything felt whole.

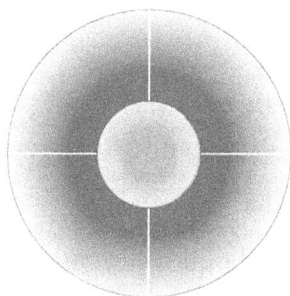

Afterword

Ben, in our story was the sage, the man who provided the wisdom and the perspective the others didn't have at the time. Ben's character was a compilation of the many people in my life who taught me how to think. That's what leaders do. They teach others how to think, so they can do what they need to do, so they can get what they want. This book is about Leadership. Leading a life well lived.

I was teaching some real estate agents a curriculum developed by Keller Williams university called Ignite. It was how to start a successful real estate career. Some of my agents came to the course multiple times so I added a one-hour session prior to the class and called it Focus on Success. The purpose of the class was to help them build their business after they had learned the fundamentals.

One day my friend, Lori, challenged me to take the conversation to the next level.

Not sure what the next level looked like, I researched and found a quote by Eleanor Roosevelt that challenged me. The former first lady said:

- "Great minds talk about ideas.
- Average minds talk about events.
- Small minds talk about people."

Some of the agents were not just attending a class, they were taking action and experiencing success. They were the "great ones". If we were going to talk about the "next level" what would be the Big Ideas, we would talk about?

As I researched the notes and materials I had acquired over the years, I found an idea I heard from Brian Buffini. Our lives incorporate 5 areas Spiritual, Personal, Family, Financial, Community. I believed that to be true. So… what does a "successful" life look like?

I facilitated conversations with our "great minds" about the following *Big Ideas*:

- Our circle of life consists of 5 separate and interconnected areas.
- The ideal life would be abundance, in each of those areas.
- Abundance requires intentional growth.
- In each area relationships are most important.

Those "Big Ideas" are the foundation for everything my group talks about. Of course, there are other ideas that stem from these because the focus is on success. We defined success as "the progressive realization of a compelling vision and predetermined goals". Success is bigger than just making money. What's the purpose of making money? The purpose of money is to fund the ideal life. The ideal life is of course different for everyone. Every one of us has the free will to lead their life as they choose. We have choices and our lives are the result of the choices we make.

In the story we see 5 main characters in different seasons of life. Ben, an influential member of the community who has lost his wife. Marcus and Pam, grandparents who are facing a fading dream of the easy retirement they had worked to attain, and a cancer scare. Justin and Kristin who seemingly "had it made" at a young age. Throughout the story we see the value of their relationships.

One *Big Idea* is relationships are most important in each area. I believe that we are perfectly positioned to achieve in life what we are currently achieving. Determined by:

1. How we think—our perspective, our context, the filter through which we view the world.
2. The environment we create or allow around us.
3. The people we choose to spend our time with.

A wise man named Jim Rohn said "You are the average of your 5 closest friends". Parents are aware of that. Good parents help their children choose the right friends because it matters. That never changes; no matter what season of life you are in. Ben's wisdom helped others to see what they could not. A friendship that added value to each one.

As their seasons and relationships progressed, so did their understanding of abundance. Abundance requires intentional growth. We've all heard the definition of insanity, "doing the same thing and expecting different results". Kristin's friend encouraged her to see herself as capable of becoming more. She helped her see herself as a person who could use her passion for dogs and create a business. Kristin took action to do something she'd never done. Her relationship with Pam and Marcus helped her navigate the negativity that often happens when you choose to change. She intentionally met with Ben to help her think differently and make good choices. You see this story is about leadership. Leading a life well lived. Being Intentional. Making right choices.

Justin was experiencing success and then failure. The choices he made were a direct reflection of his mindset. He, like many of us, was primarily focused on one area of his life. His occupation.

When he lost his job, he pulled away from his relationship with Kristin. His "context", the filter through which he viewed the world, was that his wife loved him for what he does, not who he is. He chose to keep bad news from her assuming she would reject him. Instead, he chose alcohol as the answer. He later looked for the "easy way" by gambling. Paying attention to only one or two areas instead of all 5 can cause us to miss the bigger picture. The big picture of course is . . . this is your life. You get one shot at it. There is no rehearsal. Time marches on so what we focus on matters.

As I write this, I am in my 70's. I love my life, and like most of us there are things I would have done differently. All my choices have brought me to where I am now. I live an abundant life. More than I need financially. A wonderful family I love to spend time with. I have good health, good friends, and great relationships that add value to my life. I am grateful, however, not satisfied. The wonderful thing about abundance is there's more. More growth, more experiences, Deeper relationships. We are Made 4 More.

Leading A Life Well Lived. The key word is leading. Leadership is a skill that anyone can learn. Gary Keller, the founder of Keller Williams Realty, told me that leaders are clear about 5 things:

- Mission—the purpose, the goal, the why.
- Vision—what it looks like when the purpose is being accomplished.

- Values—what needs to be valued to achieve the Mission.

- Beliefs—the rules we use to play the game of life.

- Perspective—clarity on where you are vs. where you intend to be.

Leading a life of abundance requires clarity in each area. I'm going to refer to areas as circles. To me a circle represents something complete. You cannot tell where it starts or where it stops. The circle can always grow larger.

It's important to determine your purpose your "Why". What you were created for. The founding fathers of the United States agreed that all people are created equal and endowed by their creator, with the right to life, liberty, and pursuit of happiness. I am not aware of anything created without a purpose. Every building, every tool, every class, everything I can think of has a purpose.

Many years ago, there was a phenomenon called the Pet Rock. What is a pet? Something that brings joy and companionship. Something we care for because it adds value to our lives. Some entrepreneurs put a rock inside a fancy printed box and offered it for sale. People bought it. Why? Because it was preposterous to think that rock had any real purpose or value as a companion.

We all sense that there is a purpose in our lives. At

times we have different roles to play. Our purpose can change in each role. For example, when you become a parent your role has changed, and your purpose becomes larger than yourself. Your ultimate mission in life doesn't change. It is your life and your purpose is to live it well. Many live their life by default, accepting as fate anything that comes along, thinking that's all they get. Others lead a life they design. Good and bad stuff will come along but our mission, to fulfill our created purpose, and vision remains.

Spiritual Circle

I n the Judeo/Christian world it is written that God created man to have a relationship with his creation. We are taught that God created man in his image. What that means, among other things, that we have the ability to create. Not just instinctively like other parts of creation, intentionally. We can have a vision for something not yet real and make choices to make it become real. In the book of Genesis is the story of God communing with Adam and Eve in the garden of Eden.

- The mission/purpose was to have relationship by regular communication.
- The vision (what it looks like when the mission is

being accomplished) is Love, Peace, Joy, Harmony, Happiness, Growth.

- What were the rules? You can do everything except eat from one tree.
- Perspective - as soon as they broke the rules they hid from the relationship.

It's apparent that spiritual abundance would be experiencing love, peace, joy, harmony, real relationships and fulfillment. Notice how Kristin in the story was happy but not fulfilled. She was invited to see a bigger picture for her life by thinking differently. Something that doesn't happen without real relationships. We all have blind spots. It takes somebody else to help us see what we currently don't. Abundance in the spiritual circle includes expanding relationships with our creator, our mentors, our friends and family that help us grow and bring peace and joy to our lives.

Personal Circle

Each of us is created with a specific personality, certain gifts or abilities, and certain passions. If you have children, you see how each one exhibits different behaviors even at an early age.

As a successful real estate salesman I was recruited many years ago to join a company opening in the Phoenix area called Keller Williams. After joining I was invited to participate in a mastermind group with other top producing agents. In that group I was exposed to people and ideas significantly different than I had before. I was leading a team to serve our clients at a much higher level than I could on my own. Real Estate teams were relatively unknown to the market at that time. Much of our conversations in that group were about sharing best practices. Within about 18 months my team was celebrated as #2 in the country. Soon afterward, excited by the experience, two teammates came to me and said they were leaving to start their own teams.

Gary Keller was coaching me at the time and when I shared with him what was happening, he asked me a profound question. "So, what do you need to learn?" When I answered he said go teach what you need to learn. Other times when I was asked to speak in front of a group my heart pounded, I choked up, sweated profusely. I finished not even knowing for sure what I had just said. I argued with Gary, sharing my limited beliefs and he continued to ask the same question "So, what do you need to learn?". He arranged for me to teach the subject matter I needed to master and put me in front of 200+ people teaching a 3-day class in Houston Texas.

I chose to challenge my fear and intentionally grow by mastering the content. I went to Houston.

In a different environment outside of work, I participated in a group to determine who we were created to be. We took assessments to reveal our personalities, our gifts and our passions. To my surprise, my #1 gift or ability is Teaching. #2 is Leadership. My Passion is to use my gifts of teaching for adults as opposed to children.

The result is that I spent 25+ years as a member of the master faculty at KWU. I was living and sharing what I was created to do. As I write this, it brings me joy to think about the people who came and thanked me for adding value by helping them think differently, so they can take the actions they need to take, to create what they want to create for their life. If it was not for my relationship with Gary, I may never have been able to experience the joy of doing what I was created to do. Who you choose to be in relationship with matters.

Thank you, Gary.

By the way, you know you are doing what you were created for because it gives you energy and excitement. You look forward, with positive anticipation, to doing it. I'm sure everyone's experienced doing something that sucks the energy out of you. Leading a Life Well Lived is about being and becoming the person you were created to be.

There are many 'personality assessments" that help

you discover your natural behaviors, how you process and respond to things that happen. The goal is to increase your self-awareness. The one I used is called DISC.

Family Circle

L eading in the family circle is more than just you. The real world of having or not having Spouses, Mom's and Dad's, Brothers and Sisters, relatives close or distant affects our lives. What could abundance be with each of these possible arrangements?

I was the oldest of 5 children. My parents were strict with me and expected me to follow the rules. My independent personality conflicted with their expectations.

A parent's job is to raise children from totally dependent to become high functioning adults. Stephen Covey in his book the *7 Habits of Highly Effective People* identified the Maturity Continuum. It is a progression from Dependent to Independent and ultimately to

Interdependent. Getting older happens automatically. Becoming more mature is an intentional growth process. My vision for success in the family circle is interdependent relationships with the ones I love. That means adding value to each other's lives. Abundance would be a family who serve each other with love, gratitude and generosity.

The family is the foundation for success in life. Each generation can add value to the next. My wife and I were blessed to have her mother actively involved, helping us raise our 2 boys. She was there to help transport to sports practices and sit with piano practice time. The relationship my boys had with their grandma was deep. Interdependent relationships allow each member of the family to thrive in ways otherwise not possible.

I was privileged to be selected as a trainer for a workshop called *Fierce Conversations*. Susan Scott authored the best-selling book and the workshop. As the facilitator I experienced lives and businesses changed for people who attended. Susan said, "What gets talked about, and how it is talked about, will determine what gets done in an organization". Your family can be considered an organization. Leading the conversation to focus on healthy relationships and abundant thinking is your job. If not you, who then?

Each of us can create a vision for abundance. Leading your life is knowing your current reality in relation to what you want to accomplish and executing a plan to make your vision a new reality.

Each of us can create a vision for abundance. Leading your life is knowing your current reality in relation to what you want to accomplish and executing a plan to make your vision a new reality.

Use the QR Code to access the tools to help you get started.

Financial Circle

We create value in this world by what we choose to do. Others will pay money in return for the value we create. The big Idea here is that the purpose of money is to fund the ideal life. The life of abundance. The more value we can add to others, the more money we tend to make.

People make financial plans and goals for their business, their investments, their career. It is easy to assume that more money means a better life. It's not necessarily true, it only means more money. When you are clear about what abundance looks like in each area of life it leads to clarity on how much money will fund the vision for your ideal life.

During the Focus on Success conversations I lead, one man decided to spend a special weekend with his wife to get clear on their priorities in each circle. He reported back to the group that when they defined their ideal life in each area, they discovered they had the passive income they needed to fund it. Now clear about their priorities in each circle, they adjusted the time he spent working. He and his family are living life differently now, growing in abundance in each area and influencing others to do the same.

We all have a relationship with money. Some people have a scarcity relationship while others see it as abundantly available. Scarcity causes fear while the belief in abundance results in hope or faith. Part of effective leadership is challenging our beliefs, our truths, our attitudes and opinions. Question for you. Is the way you think about money serving or hindering your growth? The QR code below will give you a tool you can use to make some new choices.

Money has rules. When we know what the rules are and follow them, we'll have a better outcome than if we don't. There is so much to understand about money and finance more than there is space for here.

At Made4MoreBook.com you will find resources and education that will help you achieve abundance financially. Take the time to grow in your understanding of how money works. Learn from many who have already achieved financial independence.

Use the QR Code to access the tools to help you get started.

Community Circle

Our community is comprised of many things but let's just say it's the people we do life with. Depending on our personality we may enjoy lots of people or others not so much. The ideal life would include what best suits who we were created to be. Some people have lots of friends that are deal friends. These are the people in your life for whatever benefits them at the time. Customers, neighbors, clients, co-workers, you get the picture. Of course there's nothing wrong with that, it's normal.

I submit that a life well lived is more about real

friends. The people that know you and help you become better. They are willing to risk telling you what you may not want to hear. After all, B.S. in your own mind sounds like the truth. In the story we see neighbors (deal friends, people who like you until…). And neighbors who become real friends (committed to the relationship) no matter what.

Community is larger than your neighborhood. It's your occupation, your business, your church or civic organization. Abundance in this circle could look like serving those in need. It could be a promotion at work or more profitability in your business. The old proverb says, "It's more blessed to give than to receive". In other words, the receiver gains and so does the giver. Abundance comes from serving and giving to others.

I chose to follow John Maxwell, likely the most respected authority on leadership. He defines leadership as simply "Influence". In the story, Ben is well known and respected in the community. He was considered a leader. What can we learn from him? He is generous with his time, talents and resources. He spent hours with people he valued sharing the truths he learned in life. He led events at the church; he hosted parties where he invited his community. It's easy to see that his generosity comes from his gratitude. Grateful for the blessing he receives from his community relationships.

Take the chance to influence your community or business by leading a committee, a group or a team.

When you do, follow a model that has proven successful for others. You'll succeed faster. Many people choose not to get involved because "they don't have the time". That's likely because they don't know how to succeed through others. The QR code below will bring you a proven model to help you accomplish far more in less time by working with and through others in your community.

Use the QR Code to access the tools to help you get started.

Summation
Great Minds Talk About Ideas

I t starts with your mindset. What you believe to be true. It is your context, your perspective. Your context or mindset can be changed. It can be damaged, or it can be enhanced. The reality is that no matter what your age you can grow. You can become more. You and I are Made 4 More.

What is your context? What do you believe is true

and what are your opinions and your attitudes about things in each circle of life. Your context, your filter through which you experience life, will determine what you will accept and what you will reject. The bottom line is that you are perfectly positioned, to achieve in life, what you are currently achieving. Is that okay? Is it what you want? Is there more? What needs to change?

In my case I learned early in my career that the way I interacted with people was not helpful to achieve my goals. I attended a course on *Psycho-Cybernetics* a book written many years ago by Maxwell Maltz. The gist of the course was how our subconscious mind controls our thoughts and behaviors. I was introduced to a process of visualization as a vehicle to change my subconscious and how my brain processed the world around me. The exercises transformed how I perceived myself and changed the quality of my life. Some in the class used the process to quit smoking. I used it and changed my thoughts and my behaviors to achieve the success I wanted as a Realtor. It works!

Scan this QR Code to use this process for yourself.

You can change your context in any of the 5 circles. It takes work. It takes intentionally leading your life. It takes others that add value to your life by helping you think bigger. Look for those people and build relationships with them.

My definition of Abundance is: Having everything I need... and there's more.

Abundance is the opposite of scarcity. Scarcity thinking causes people to hoard and hold on to things. They are fearful, afraid of losing, afraid there is not enough. Abundant thinking causes us to embrace growth. We know there is more, that's faith, not fear. Both faith and fear are the certainty of what has not yet happened. We are told in the scriptures that God did not create us with a spirit of fear. (2 Timothy 1:7). Our creator wants us to have life abundantly.

One more thought about the ideal abundant life. When we take time to evaluate our lives, we all have much to be grateful for. If you ask someone what they are grateful for, they will talk about relationships and what makes them happy. Abundant thinking includes gratitude, growth, and generosity.

Gratitude is about me. You hear it in the words I am grateful for _____
(fill in the blank). Gratitude is internal, it's about me. Gratitude is good. Science has proven that gratitude is a bridge to happiness.

Growth is necessary for abundance. It is expected, it is desired, and it is to be pursued.

Generosity is the outward expression of gratitude and growth. Generosity is not about me; it is about blessing and adding value to others. Some call it "Givers Gain." Generosity is demonstrated by sharing your time, your talents, and your resources. In the story Ben was a happy, grateful, and generous man who became happier by sharing with others.

Life is comprised of 5 separate and interconnected circles. The Ideal Life is Abundance in each circle. In each circle relationships matter most. Abundance requires intentional growth. I pray that these ideas, ideas great people talk about, will add value to your life and the others around you.

Do not let these Big Ideas stop here. Become part of our community at Made4MoreBook.com

About the Author
Steve Chader

Steve Chader has been a leader in the Arizona real estate industry since 1977. Founder of Keller Williams Integrity First Realty, one of REAL Trends top 350 real estate companies in the U.S. He is also general partner of TCT Property Management Services, managing over 500 single-family homes and more than 60 commercial properties.

Recognized as a "Top 1% Realtor®" in the United States, Steve was honored with the Residential Real Estate Lifetime Achievement Award by the Phoenix Business Journal. He was also selected as "Realtor of the Year" from his 11,000 member realtor association.

Steve co-authored the national bestselling book, *HOLD, How to Find, Buy and Rent Houses for Wealth*. The book reveals the safe, simple, secure strategy to build wealth with real estate. He and his co authors have helped thousands of people create financial security.

amazon.com/HOLD-Find-Rent-Houses-Wealth/dp/0071797041/

Steve served his community in various capacities including as Town Council member for Gilbert, AZ., Master faculty member at Keller Williams University. Ordained as an elder in the Presbyterian Church of America. A father of two, and grandfather of three boys. Steve also enjoys playing the bass guitar with his classic rock band, Group Therapy, "having fun playing music for people having fun."